MW00996799

CONTEMPORARY CLASSICAL

CONTEMPORARY CLASSICAL

The Architecture of Andrew Skurman

Andrew Skurman

PRINCETON ARCHITECTURAL PRESS NEW YORK

Published by
Princeton Architectural Press
37 East Seventh Street
New York, New York 10003

Visit our website at www.papress.com.

© 2012 Princeton Architectural Press
All rights reserved
Printed and bound in China
15 14 13 12 4 3 2 1 First edition

No part of this book may be used or reproduced in any manner without written permission from the publisher, except in the context of reviews.

Every reasonable attempt has been made to identify owners of copyright. Errors or omissions will be corrected in subsequent editions.

Editor: Dan Simon
Design: Doug Turshen with David Huang

Special thanks to: Bree Anne Apperley, Sara Bader, Janet Behning, Nicola Bednarek Brower, Fannie Bushin, Megan Carey, Carina Cha, Andrea Chlad, Russell Fernandez, Will Foster, Jan Haux, Diane Levinson, Jennifer Lippert, Gina Morrow, Katharine Myers, John Myers, Margaret Rogalski, Elana Schlenker, Sara Stemen, Paul Wagner, and Joseph Weston of Princeton Architectural Press —Kevin C. Lippert, publisher

Library of Congress Cataloging-in-Publication Data

Skurman, Andrew, 1953–
Contemporary classical: the architecture of Andrew Skurman / by Andrew Skurman. — First edition.
pages cm
Includes bibliographical references.
ISBN 978-1-61689-088-9 (alk. paper)
1. Skurman, Andrew, 1953–Theme, motives 2. Architecture, Domestic—United States. 3. Classicism in architecture—United States. I. Title. II. Title: Architecture of Andrew Skurman.
NA737.S533A35 2012
728.092—dc23
                                        2011052897

Overleaf: Entry door at A Country House
Opposite: Wedding pavilion at The Resort at Pelican Hill

This book is dedicated to my wife,

Françoise Jaudel Skurman,

*with gratitude for her loving support,
council, and encouragement.*

Opposite page: Enfilade entry at A Country House
Following page: Dining pavilion at A Hillside Villa

TABLE OF CONTENTS

FOREWORD
by Diane Lewis

I HOPE THAT THIS INTRODUCTION CAN contribute insight and background on the work of Andrew Skurman through the attributes which I have witnessed and reflected upon since 1974. There are some aspects of his process, his thought, his roots, and the struggle of the period in which we have practiced that deserve some light, especially upon the publication of this extensive compendium of selections from his constructed work. This book forcefully and clearly tells one story about his accomplishments, but I will tell another story, that perhaps photographs of buildings do not, or cannot, serve.

My line on his work is about his natural ability and commitment to impart the touch, refinement, lightness, and solidity of his drawings, his ideas, and his sense of history to his architecture. This particular architectural touch contains what I would call a genetic depth of craftsmanship, and has been inspired by his continuous and passionate engagement with the love and observation of painting.

From the first, his unique hand was apparent. Known as a uniquely brilliant draftsman in the days of our architectural education together at Cooper Union in the 1970s, this rapid-fire sensibility was acknowledged and appreciated into the period when we both worked at I. M. Pei and Partners, as well as the years he spent at Skidmore, Owings & Merrill. His virtuosity at exploding the concept in drawing is a vehicle which allows him to continue to express and develop the powerful voids and solids that comprise his approach to both the domestic and the civic domains.

In my memory Skurman would be seen, and will always be pictured, sitting with an introspective intensity at the studio desk, lost in thought, staring into another space with an existential discomfort. These periods are always dramatically broken with an apparent epiphany, when he seems to brim over with a critical mass of conceptualized form and a mobilizing bolt of energy.

Then the action begins, accompanied by a beautiful sandy sound that allows those around him to hear him, pen or pencil in hand, slicing space with the dry incisive line he can thoughtfully project on the page. Innately desirous of an elegant, taut quality of construction—

sustained throughout his architectural life into the projects of this book—he carefully cuts the page with boundaries and asserts seams and spans. His is a classic architectural sense of what I call "the tailoring" of detail, walls, edges, orders, entries, ambulatories, and materials in those hard, thin incisive lines.

For Skurman the project—each project—comes to fruition almost at once. Lines of light defining space. A collage he once made, inspired by *Violon et Guitare* by Juan Gris, folded and cut simply of only white paper, sliced in the manner in which he draws, was and remains the opening salvo of his style. Luminous relief achieved from direct conceptual and physical

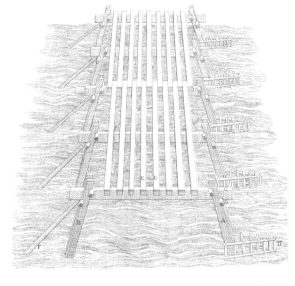

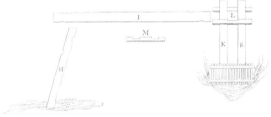

engagement with the material at hand is the character of his touch. This ability is critical to the discipline of architecture, and is the deepest root of the classical.

There is a dramatic interdependence between the austere and the voluptuous in

Skurman's work. His experiments with materials and collisions of style are reflected in his selection, fabrication, and placement of certain works of art, objects, and materials that surround him. His approach to the issue of cultural memory and the challenge of historic precedent in architecture is uniquely embodied in his process.

He has a way of receiving serendipitous inspiration from architecture of all epochs. Most interesting was the time he telephoned me to marvel about his affinity for a Palladio drawing of a bridge. He told me that from the drawing, he could "read" a great span condition for a table. He was able to derive a structural posture and invent subtle details of connection from this sixteenth-century drawing with which he developed elegant furniture, catching a new essence of Palladio's character.

I choose to focus on this particular transformation because it requires a suspension of the historicist tendency. This locates Skurman's work in a different domain than that of imitation or stylistic academicism. Much of his work, and the struggle he has chosen to take on in regard to historic orders and forms, is one of trying to capture the spatial spirit of the architectural precedents that fascinate him.

Today, a challenge resides in the contemporary American approach to functionalism that confronts the scale and the platonic purity of the precedents that attract Skurman's interest and inspire his forms. Here is an architect whose projects are a symphony of definitive voids, ambulatories, and volumes in light. The lingering question about the future of his work is whether he can invest this program with the cultural refinement of the tectonics that his projects provide. Their style is a manifestation of the era and geography of his practice. His imagination, ability, and philosophical search give him the ability to enter new territory with the publication of this book.

His interest in refined fabrication has manifested itself in many diverse tectonic visions. One specific legacy that I see in his work, and that positions his objectives out of time and the limits of style, is an innate sense of the marquetry and the inlay of architectural cabinetry in the Viennese tradition. This is probably why I have always felt his tone to be entwined with that of Loos. The early twentieth-century work which integrated the mystery of rich materiality and the memory of palatial symphonies of texture, weights, finish, and reflection, through an austere tectonic hierarchy of elements is the very talent with which Andrew Skurman shapes his architecture. Like the leather box which he keeps on his desk, an elegant silence and an inner world is wrapped in a tactile sculptural exterior. He works and projects his vision with a sense of stability and peace. His imagination of the ideal and the weight of the Classical has characterized the work he creates with enormous but quiet dignity and drive.

INTRODUCTION

W<small>HEN NEW CLIENTS FIRST COME TO MY</small> office and describe the house they want to build, they often bring with them a collection of pictures that express their initial ideas. I then pull books from a library in the conference room of our office that encompasses nearly every kind of classical architecture. In this way, by putting the perfect precedents side by side, the conception of the house is formed. The clients' favorite pictures and the color photocopies of the precedents form the beginning of a project binder that grows and changes as the building design develops.

I am inspired by a wide range of classical architecture, as American classicists traditionally have been. Greece, Rome, and the pre-Modern architects of Western Europe are always present in my mind. Whenever a client picks a certain building character or form, we study the architecture of that time and place and do our best to achieve an accurate, yet contemporary representation of the style. The work we do is directly inspired by the extraordinary beauty and harmony of existing architecture.

We study the exterior rhythm, structure, interior circulation, and disposition of rooms which are worked out in a way to give the impression of effortless harmony within historical plans. We simultaneously conceive the elevations, working with all possible architectural orders, especially those after Serlio, Palladio, and Vignola. Though I deeply admire and respect the classical orders, they are often altered according to our needs. For example, at The Resort at Pelican Hill (2009) in Southern California, we used the Palladian Doric order, but the base of that order was too highly articulated for our needs, so we used the base of Palladio's Tuscan order instead.

Pelican Hill expresses how we work: we always refer to a precedent and we always feel free to create a variation. When Greek ruins were unearthed, everything was found to be exquisitely beautiful, retaining its beauty all those centuries later, even amid modern sensibilities. Now we have the technology to copy it all perfectly, but our eyes have adjusted to

Opposite: Renovation of a Julia Morgan apartment

a less-ornamented world, making selective omission and aesthetic choices vital to the success of a project.

I had decided to be an architect when I was 12. As a sixth grader, I excelled at art and my teacher thought I should pursue my talent in junior high school and eventually become an artist. Having been lucky enough to have two architects in the family who were knowledgeable about the profession, I chose instead to pursue architecture, becoming obsessed with mechanical drafting in junior high and high school.

My first professional encounter with architecture came at a young age. I was adamant about not returning to summer camp, which my brother and all the other kids loved. My family, who didn't know what to do with me, sent me to work with my grandfather Louis. He owned an elevator company in New York called Parkline Elevator Cabs. I spent my summer days drawing both modern elevators and

Above: An art collector's apartment *Opposite:* A Georgian library

classical ones with wood paneling for buildings all over the country. My grandfather Lou was proud of me, and I briefly considered going into industrial engineering to work in his business.

Lou was a brilliant man with many patents to his name, but his behavior tended toward the absent-minded professor type. He once had an appointment with Philip Johnson (who designed the Seagram Building with Mies van der Rohe), and was told that he should dress properly for the meeting, and so he did. When he arrived, Johnson asked, "Lou, what's wrong? You look faint, why don't you loosen your tie." My grandfather had put on two shirts and two ties.

Through a weekend program I found fantastic joy and discoveries at the museums in New York, including the Museum of Modern Art, the Whitney, the Met, and the Frick. I loved both the modern and the classical museum architecture and frequented the galleries of decorative arts where I was fascinated by both the new and historical objects. I adored the period rooms, and would often pace up and down the

galleries of fine art for several hours straight, admiring the ever-evolving selection of canvases and sculptures.

Architecture ran in the family. Changes to the layout of the city of New York belonged to my great-uncle Joe, an architect who had attended Columbia University. He was the chairman of the Board of Standards and Appeals for the City of New York, ruling on all building variances for 25 years. He received a gold badge equivalent to that of the Commissioner of Police, a chauffeur driven car, and exemption from all tolls. He was said to be extremely honest, never allowing an undeserved variance. It was probably true, as he was originally appointed by Mayor Wagner with successive appointments by Lindsay, Beame, and Koch, and never became wealthy. As a child I loved attending his swearing-ins. They always took place in the beautiful Georgian ballroom at Gracie Mansion, the Mayor's residence. I was there for the first time in 1966 when Mott Schmidt had recently completed the Susan B. Wagner wing, his last major commission, at the age of 77. Now one of my favorite classical architects, at the time, I had no idea who he was.

I went to the Cooper Union School of Architecture and, as did all students who went to school in the 1970s, I studied modern architecture. The living god of the department was John Hejduk, a brilliant theoretical architect with the ability to design things that no one had ever seen. He was a genius at encouraging and stimulating our creativity. We lived by the rules and works of Mies van der Rohe and Alvar Aalto, but our hero was the Swiss-born Le Corbusier, who was naturalized as a Frenchman in 1930. In addition to being an architect, Le Corbusier was an urban planner, painter, sculptor, writer, and furniture designer. His ambitions were huge: he believed in using modern industrial techniques and strategies to allow cities to evolve into more efficient environments with higher standards of living for their inhabitants. But our true inspiration was the poetry of Le Corbusier's forms.

My first job out of school was with I. M. Pei and Partners, where I worked on the design of office buildings and, in a very modest way, on museums. My most important job under Pei was at the Boston Museum of Fine Arts, where I designed the Asian curator's rooms.

I moved to San Francisco in 1981, working at the two most prominent firms in that city: I was at Skidmore, Owings & Merrill from 1981 to 1987, where I learned how to be in charge of a large commercial project and interact with the client. In 1987, I joined Gensler and Associates, where working as a studio director I learned to apply my SOM experience, managing a design studio with numerous projects and clients.

Opposite: A new family room for a Julia Morgan apartment

19

During my time at SOM, a Chicago industrialist came to the San Francisco office to commission a large, very modern home on the bay in Belvedere. I had been appointed the project architect, beginning an entirely new and different career within the field of architecture. After having spent 15 years pursuing a career in commercial modern architecture, I made the conscious decision to reinvent myself within the field, opening an office specializing in my other early inspiration: classical architecture. In 1992, I started my own practice.

I BELIEVE THAT A HOUSE WANTS TO BE comfortable and welcoming, to express the history of the family, present, past, and future. Classicism is an expression of this passing of the generations. If one builds a home, it is compelling to think of it lasting for eternity, both as a work of art and as a sanctuary from the outside world, surrounding you in the warm splendor and beautiful proportions of its classical lines. Philip Johnson said it it in a nutshell:

> *I am a modern architect, a product of the continually evolving Western humanist tradition. . . . Of all the architectural methodologies yet evolved, I believe classicism best reconciles the idiosyncrasies of the local, the immediate and the expedient with the grand, the ennobling and enduring values that draw people together in their diversity. . . . Classicism offers the architect a canon, but what a liberal and tolerant canon it is.*

I wanted to build beautiful private homes in the language of classical architecture, to interact with my clients and help them with their aesthetic choices and functional needs. I thrive on the tension that always exists between the architect and the client. It's such an old and eternal question that it was even described at length by Aristotle three centuries before our era:

> *The architect, he says in substance, is the artist and the expert, the only one who knows what his work aims at and how it should be executed. He owns the best knowledge, the complete knowledge. But, adds Aristotle, the architect does not have the right to decide alone. Because the person who uses the house, even though he or she is not an expert, is entitled to make a judgment about it, even more so than the architect.*

My main inspiration is the ongoing trace of Palladian architecture. In the sixteenth century, Andrea Palladio studied the principals of the architecture of ancient Rome and wrote his *Quattro Libri dell'Architettura*. These treatises traveled all over the world, making Palladio the father of modern classicism. Ever since that time, architects have adjusted the forms and orders described in his four books to the local climate, topography, and tastes of their clients.

In the early nineteenth century, a number of particularly graceful and light interpretations of Palladian designs were built that directly befit our present age. Among my favorite pieces of architecture from that time is a set of four houses by Karl Friedrich Schinkel, restored to their original condition in Berlin and in nearby Potsdam. In those days, Prussia was not a wealthy country; nevertheless, Schinkel was able to convey a sense of supreme elegance in his architecture. Paneling and crown moldings, for instance, are painted on, rather than applied three-dimensionally. In one of these houses, his Schloss Tegel, a collection of over-scaled, white plaster classical figurative sculptures are displayed. It's about doing more with less. Today, heavily ornamented rooms look old fashioned, and we love to exercise restraint in our desire for magnificence, but the size of these houses is modern and modest by today's standards at approximately 3,500 square feet with symmetrical floor plans.

Above: Renovation of a Julia Morgan apartment

Another favorite motif of mine is the French use of round and oval forms, not only for windows but also for the design of rooms. I'm a great proponent of poché spaces: these are the spaces in between that allow for rooms of pure geometric shapes. This lost space allows for better and more graceful circulation in addition to the creation of rooms of pure form, a concept borrowed from ancient Rome.

I also love the French use of mirrors placed opposite exterior walls to reflect daylight and views; curvaceous, Louis XV–wrought iron balustrades; and parquet de Versailles oak floors. I admire the mansard roof and find it very useful where the height of buildings is limited, allowing the creation of another livable level with no added height. The roofline remains sloped, but is angled until almost vertical, while dormer windows provide air and light to the interior.

GEORGIAN ARCHITECTURE HOLDS ESPECIALLY true to Palladio, and is loved throughout America where construction in brick and wood is often preferred over stone. The restraint and understatement inherent to this style speaks to the modernist in me, where a decorative cornice and columnar entry portico might make up the only highly classical or detailed elements on the facade.

I feel that images are the inspirational representations of architecture, for instance *The Ideal City* by Piero della Francesca. This painting makes me think of the house as a small but important contribution to the city, a place where an enlightened consciousness contributes to the life and development of the community. And there are other artists who inspire me: when I am given the chance to design a house next to the water, images of Venice by Turner and Canaletto are always on my mind. Alternately, when I create a house in the countryside, I am aware that this dwelling is not only a place where a family will live, but a place where it will evolve and provide an education to the next generation.

I sometimes wonder about the future of my houses, asking what will become of them as time passes. I hope that the children who grow up in them will remember their childhood homes as places of beauty and comfort; I hope that local planning commissions will take good care of the architecture; and I hope that the families that dwell within will be remembered for having lived there in happiness.

Opposite: Entrance gallery in a pied-à-terre

MEDITERRANEAN ARCHITECTURE

Mediterranean architecture encompasses the character of a great many countries, regions, and time periods. Used today, the Western classical traditions that began in Greece—columnar orders, pediments, and acroteria juxtaposed against stone and plaster walls—can transport visitors back to antiquity.

Italy inherited the wealth of Greek architecture and culture and reared a group of architects whose influence can be seen worldwide. Alberti, Serlio, Michelangelo, and Scamozzi would all agree with Palladio's words in the *Quattro Libri* that "Beauty shall result from order and from the relationship of the whole to the individual parts, of the parts to each other and of the parts back to the whole." Classical orders, axes, and rooms of pure geometric forms abound in the various forms of Italian classicism.

In Spain, the Alhambra is a beautiful example of formal design, while the provincial houses and *cortijos* (farm houses) of Andalusia exemplify the informal aspects of the region. The Spanish Colonial style in the southwestern United States is derived from these building traditions of southern Spain.

A HILLSIDE VILLA

Amultitude of objects collected by the owner can be found throughout this large, comfortable house. The client had fallen in love with the site, which was located on a hillside, and purchased the land the same day she toured it. She wanted to build a house on it that would feel like a 1920s Spanish Colonial residence, set deep in the woods on a hilltop. I created a house that would do so while also serving as a repository and exhibition space for her art collection—a Mediterranean house revisited by an eclectic mind.

A large living room was placed next to a warm, wooden kitchen, where it serves as the main gathering space in the house [*p. 29, Fig. 5*]. This enormous space is roofed with exposed timber trusses, reminiscent of the 1920 interior of the George Washington Smith Residence No. 2 (1920) in Montecito, California [*p. 32, Fig. 7*]. Two eighteenth-century Italian gesso columns frame the doorway to this space while a sixteenth-century fireplace bought at a Parisian flea market sits centered on the far

Left: Stair from the Hôtel de Beauvais, Paris, France, 1656, Antoine le Pautre
Opposite: View of the stair from above

26

wall, bringing the client's collection directly into the architecture [*p. 33*]. To fit the drama and scale of the space, French door assemblies with arched transoms were designed to create a grand, well-lit, dramatic space for entertaining [*p. 29, Fig. 4*]. In order to keep the space from becoming overwhelming, my longtime collaborator, interior designer Suzanne Tucker, arranged the furniture in such a way that the seating was grouped into three distinct seating areas. This breaks it up, and allows the client to comfortably entertain both small and large groups in the same area. A stair designed for the space is similar to the stair at the Hôtel de Beauvais (1656) in Paris by Antoine le Pautre [*p. 26; p. 27*].

By creating this very large living room, the client sacrificed the space that would otherwise have made up a dining room. An outdoor dining pavilion was created in place of a traditional dining room [*pp. 30–31*]. The loggia is delimited by two rows of Doric columns with a full entablature above, each supporting three arches, similar to the portico at the Il Palmetto (1930) in Palm Beach by Maurice Fatio [*p. 28, Fig. 1*]. The space is roofed, with a barrel vault finished in a Pompeian-red Venetian plaster to offset the interior from the cast stone and sandstone-colored integral plaster exterior. A large antique fireplace along with radiant-heat limestone floors and a custom-designed heated dining table keep the space warm during cool nights, creating a charming exterior dining terrace with romantic views of the gardens usable year round.

1

2

Fig. 1: Outdoor pavilion at Il Palmetto, Palm Beach, Florida, 1930, Maurice Fatio
Fig. 2: Arched door with a view of the pool and gardens *Fig. 3:* Living room
Fig. 4: View out the arched French doors from the living room *Fig. 5:* View of the villa from the auto court

3

4

5

The outdoor dining pavilion, with a barrel vault finished in a Pompeian-red Venetian plaster supported by arches above Doric cast stone columns. The dining table and flooring were custom designed with radiant heating for cool nights.

6

7

8

Fig. 6: Master bedroom *Fig. 7:* Interior room of the George Washington Smith Residence No. 2, Montecito, California, 1920, George Washington Smith *Fig. 8:* View into the master bath
Opposite: View from the living room of the eighteenth-century gesso columns at the gallery doorway

A GREEK VILLA

T HIS HOUSE'S DESIGN REFLECTS ANCIENT GREEK tradition that meets twenty-first-century needs and desires. Built for a Greek-American family, many of the elements of high classical Greek architecture are found throughout the house, be they intricate mosaic floors, pedimented volumes, finials, acroteria, or wooden doors with intricate bronze hardware. The Villa Kérylos (1908) in Beaulieu-sur-Mer, built by Théodore Reinach, inspired these elements. An erudite nineteenth-century scholar of ancient Greece, Reinach used his family's fortune to build a perfect example of an inherently Greek house, employing the architect and director of the École nationale supérieure des beaux-arts, Emmanuel Pontremolli. While the Villa Kérylos is now a museum, this project is a modern homeowner's dream of luxury and elegance.

This project began as a renovation. As the design evolved, the client decided to demolish the house and build a new one on the the old foundations. As construction commenced, we found that the foundations were inadequate. Since the construction documents were already finished, we decided to pour the new foundations in the same location as those already existing.

The house is approached through a long hedge-bordered driveway that culminates in an octagonal auto court that intentionally obscures the view of the gardens around the house. The entry to the house is a circular, domed portico reminiscent of a garden folly or the 1816 central entry portico of Tudor Place in Washington, DC, designed by William Thornton [*p. 39, Figs. 1–3*]. Radial beams protrude from the circular entablature, becoming trellises. The entrance is inspired by the door at the Villa Kérylos [*p. 39, Fig. 4*]. Locating the entry at the convergence of two wings of the house creates a distinctly powerful moment [*p. 35*].

The clients wanted the house to be only one level, uncharacteristic for such a large house, so the design required an elaborate circulation sequence. Upon entering the portico and passing through to the entrance hall, visitors can either move along the cross-axis into the living or dining room, or

Opposite: Entry portico

34

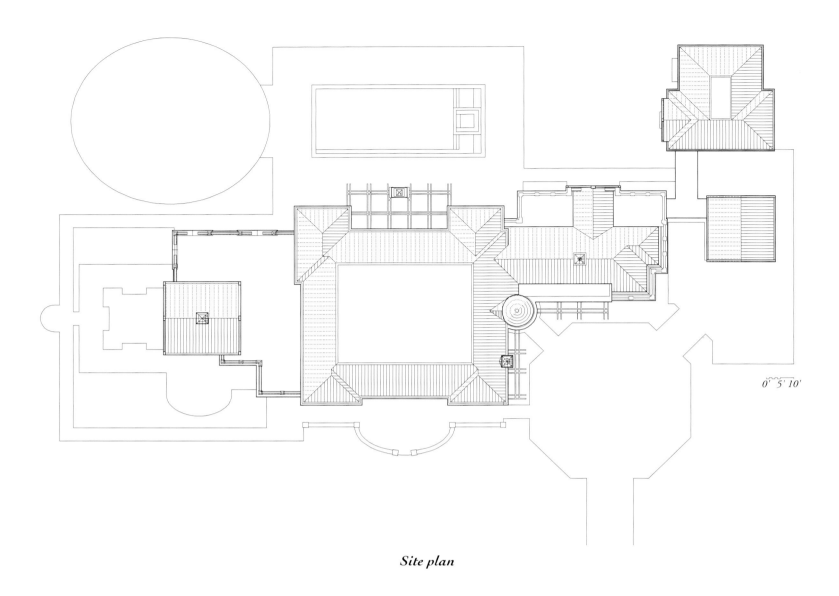

Site plan

continue through to the family room or gallery beyond [*p. 41; pp. 42–43*]. The gallery, lined with Doric pilasters with lay lights above and a mosaic floor below, culminates in a niche with a statue of a nymph [*p. 49; p. 50, Fig. 11*]. The bedrooms are accessed off of this dynamic space. The master bedroom, with interior design by Suzanne Tucker, is found through a vestibule adjacent to the terminating niche. When one moves into a room off the gallery, the gardens are finally revealed; the viewer will perceive the site to be far larger than it actually is.

The elevations are punctuated by the use of various material treatments. The plaster with stone quoining is contrasted with full-height rusticated stone cladding on different portions of the facade [*pp. 44–45; p. 54*]. This was drawn from Robert Adam's Kenwood at Hampstead Heath (1760) which also served as inspiration for the Serlian windows used throughout and for details present on the entry doorway surrounds. The contrast between the smooth plaster and large, rusticated blocks breaks up the house into smaller portions, relieving what might otherwise be a massive facade.

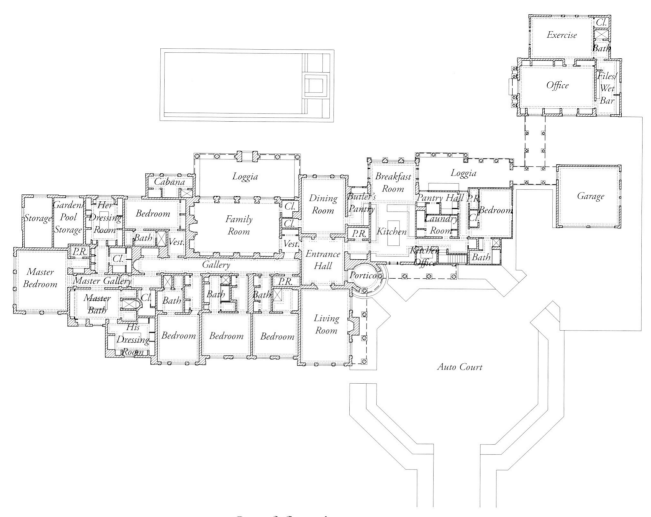

Ground floor plan

The master bedroom, located at the end of the house, presents a powerful facade [*p. 46; p. 47*]. Three arches fall upon pilasters embedded in the building while a Doric denticulated entablature marches along the top of the elevation with a pediment capping the rectilinear form. Acroteria based upon those found at the Temple of Zeus at Nemea (built circa 300 BCE) accentuate the composition [*p. 50, Fig. 9*].

The distinctions between various elements of the elevation retain a sense of unity, but also apply to the rear elevation. The cabana and dining room have Serlian windows, and are stepped back from the family room's trellised portico. The lightness of this portion of the house is contrasted with Doric columns supporting a full entablature with a balustrade above at the breakfast nook and portico. A pavilion set apart from the main house is centered to create a view out over the pool. It has a large doorway with two Doric columns supporting a broken triangular pediment that is framed by cypress trees, creating the sense of an ancient Roman natatio [*pp. 52–55*].

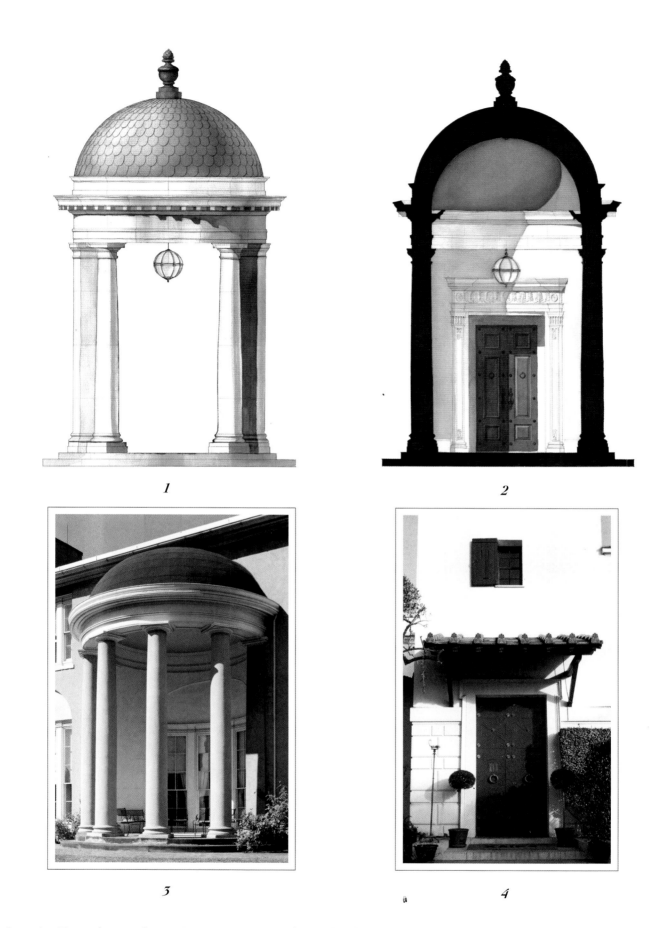

1

2

3

4

Opposite: Entry door at the portico *Fig. 1:* Watercolor study of the entry portico *Fig. 2:* Watercolor study in section
Fig. 3: Front entry of Tudor Place, Georgetown, Washington, DC, 1816, William Thornton
Fig. 4: Entry door at the Villa Kérylos, Beaulieu-sur-Mer, France, 1908, Théodore Reinach

5

6

7

8

Fig. 5: Capital from the Tower of the Winds in Athens, Greece, first century BCE, Andronicus Cyrrhestes
Fig. 6: Door from the north portico of the Erechtheum in Athens, Greece, 421–406 BCE, Mnesicles
Fig. 7: View of the entry door from the entrance hall   *Fig. 8:* Watercolor study of an interior door
Opposite: View of the interior doorway from the entrance hall to the living room

40

The double-height
living room

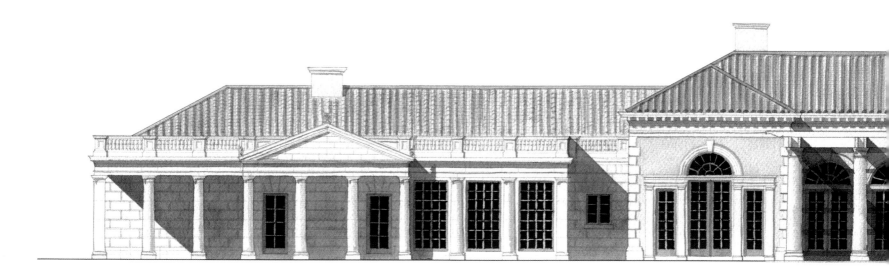

Watercolor study of the rear garden facade

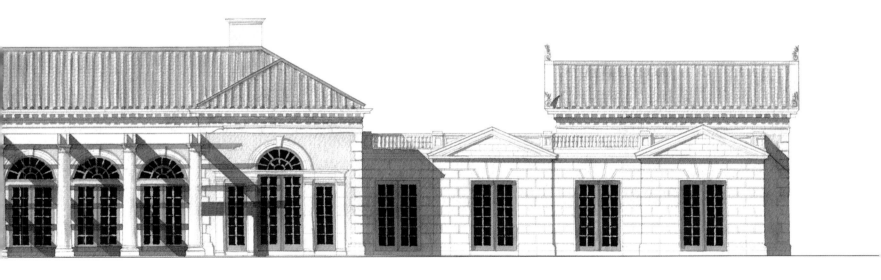

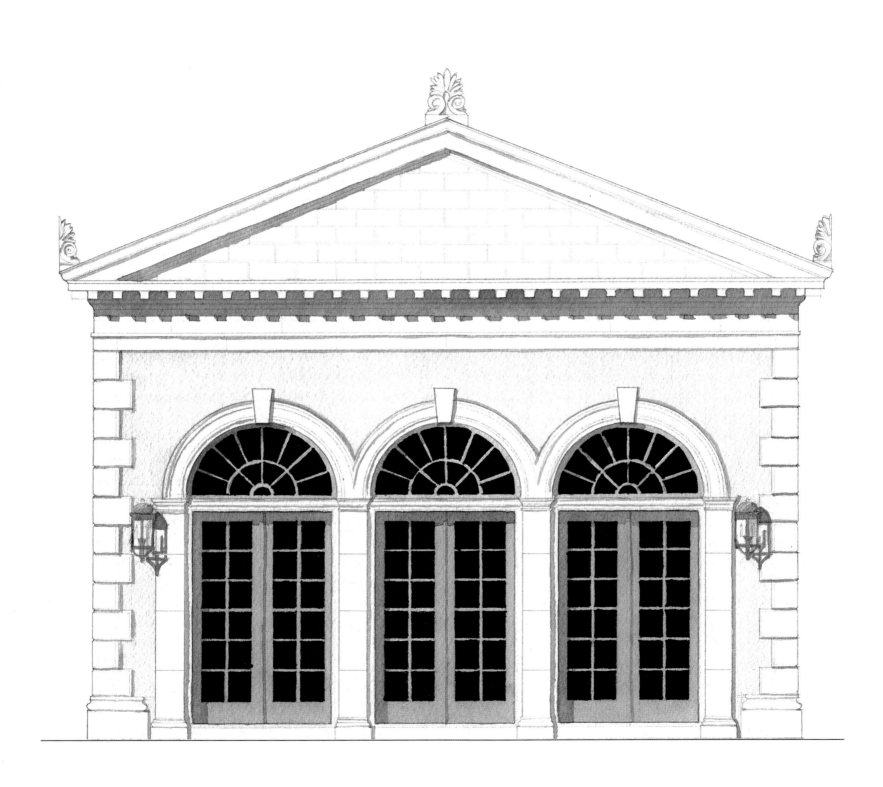

Above: Watercolor study of the master bedroom facade *Opposite:* Detail of the master bedroom elevation

Above: Master bedroom *Below:* Master bath *Opposite:* View of the gallery

48

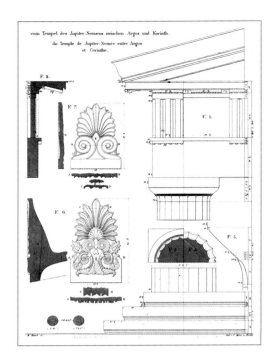

9

10

11

12

Fig. 9: Acroterion from the Temple of Zeus at Nemea, Greece, ca. 330 BCE
Fig. 10: Andron of the Villa Kérylos, Beaulieu-sur-Mer, France, 1908, Emmanuel Pontremoli *Fig. 11:* View of the gallery looking back towards the entrance hall *Fig. 12:* Detailed view of walnut paneling in the family room
Opposite: Family room *Following pages:* View across the pool to the office pavilion

13

14

15

Fig. 13: View of the front facade *Fig. 14:* View of the master bedroom wing
Fig. 15: Detail of her dressing room elevation *Opposite:* Loggia

AN ITALIANATE LAKESIDE VILLA

THIS LAKESIDE VILLA SITS ON A SPECTACULAR SITE located on the side of a coastal hill so steep that a road could not be built down its locations at the water's edge [*p. 57*]. To access the house, a Swiss gondola was added; it can reach the peaceful blue water in only one and a half minutes. An entry vestibule at street level, adjacent to the garage, serves as the gondola's base station [*p. 58*]. Lush vegetation shields the view of the house, creating an exciting entry sequence as the residence is revealed while the gondola descends the slope. Needless to say, the house has perfect privacy.

With such an amazing location for their home, the clients wanted a house that would evoke the feeling of an Italian villa and allow immediate access to the natural world surrounding it. We studied imagery from the Italian lake region and came up with a sophisticated design that captured the characteristics of these locales. Arched windows allow grand views from the rooms, with interior designs by Brian Murphy [*pp. 60–61; p. 62*]. Exposed-wood rafter tails, simple detailing, reclaimed European roof tiles, intricate Italian parquet floors, stone, and integral colored plaster give the building an Old World feel. A large battered base grounds the composition and creates a rustic sense of permanence and authenticity. A sizeable terrace was articulated as a bridge and built next to the house to create a spacious area for outdoor entertaining. It offers great views of the water and leads to a path that winds its way up through the landscape to the street above.

Because the site is so far below a very narrow country road, it was impossible to use trucks to offload materials at the street level. Instead, barges or helicopters were utilized to deliver the majority of the building materials, adding significant complexity to the construction process.

Opposite: Aerial view of the villa

Above: Entry vestibule at the top of the site
Opposite: View from the lower terrace

Living room

1

2

3

Fig. 1: View from a
dining room window
Fig. 2: Interior door
detail
Fig. 3: Kitchen
Opposite: View from
the living room

A SPANISH COLONIAL ESTATE
Under Construction

THE CLIENTS FOR THIS PROJECT PRESENTED US with an ambitious program and an inspiring location. They had assembled a large site by purchasing three contiguous parcels of land near the top of a hillside. The view overlooks water to a mountain top in the distance. I immediately thought of many Italian villas that utilized a series of terraces with fountains to create an axial view from the main house out to a remote point in the landscape. This concept helped formulate the overall design of the project, and became the view one sees upon entering the house.

If California can be said to have an "indigenous" style, it would be Spanish Colonial. Although the Spanish Baroque found in Latin-American countries overflows with complex sculpture, this orderly home is inspired by the Pazo de Oca (1783) in Galicia, Spain [*p. 74, Fig. 8*]. One of the most historically important buildings in Spain, it belonged to the Spanish crown under King Philip II, who built the Escurial palace and monastery upon the ruins of a twelfth-century fortress. In this Californian house, the subdued design gives precedence to the gardens and the surrounding nature, becoming a driving force in the overall scheme and style of the residence.

Having had the opportunity to work on the renovation of a George Washington Smith residence, we were able to use that house's original construction drawings at the George Washington Smith Archive in Santa Barbara as inspiration for our detailing throughout the project. We also used a set of details and photographs of fifteenth- through seventeenth-century Spanish architecture from our library for precedents [*p. 72, Figs. 1 and 2*]. By combining this Spanish Colonial detailing with Palladian axial relationships and massing, we were able to create a "Spalladian" residence, similar to the Sotto il Monte (1928) in Santa Barbara by George Washington Smith [*p. 72, Fig. 4*]. The rigorous axes present in Palladian architecture were chosen over the more informal, village-like layout often associated with the Spanish style, due to the fact that the site demanded a major axis to celebrate the glorious view.

Opposite: Site plan

64

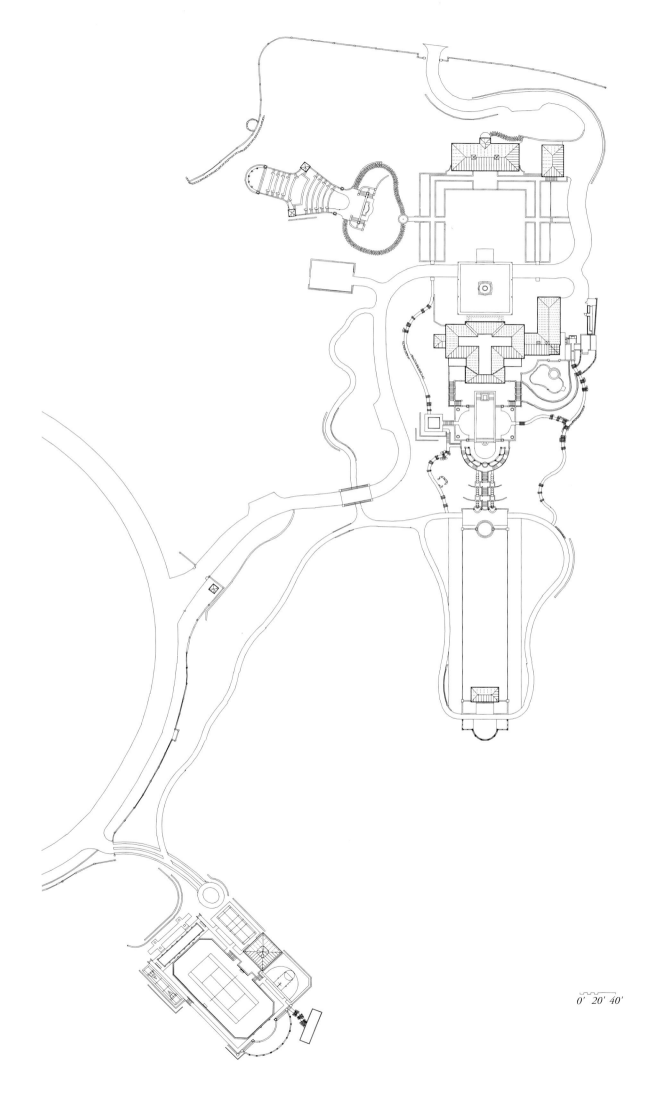

0' 20' 40'

Through the large, arched windows of the great hall located on axis with the entry hall, one gets a bird's eye view of the water and the hills beyond [*p. 73, Fig. 6*]. These same windows look out onto a sequence of terraces below, with water flowing along the center. The house steps down a full level to a pool terrace with a semicircular platform where stairs wrap around both sides, allowing access below to another terrace with a grotto [*pp. 70–71*]. The grotto is a spring point, from which a stepped sculptural shell fountain—designed by Todd Cole and inspired by those at the Casa Bienvenida (1931) in Santa Barbara by George Washington Smith—cascades alongside a descending stair [*p. 66*]. The water flowers into a long reflecting pool with an open air pavilion at the opposite end, a focal point in the foreground of the view.

In keeping with the client's desire for the house to feel established in its setting, a long winding road leads up to the auto court. The road intentionally crosses a ravine, offering the opportunity to create a bridge and adding to the feeling that the road had developed naturally over time. The bridge is designed to rattle when one drives over it, making it feel old and authentic.

Cars arrive at the auto court on axis with the main residence and the guest house which contains interior design by Suzanne Tucker. The guest house, located on the auto court opposite the main house, functions as a retaining wall as it steps down the hillside [*p. 74, Fig. 9*]. The architectural design of this building was inspired by the Kern House (1925) by George Washington Smith in Holmby Hills, California [*p. 74, Fig. 7*]. The urban containment of the auto court, along with the arched columnar screen on the lower level of the guest house with glass windows above, creates a Spanish courtyard–like feel, also inspired by the Pazo de Oca [*p. 75*].

Casa Bienvenida,
Santa Barbara, 1931,
Addison Mizner

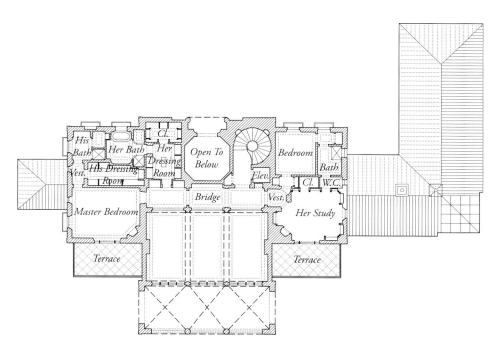

First floor plan

His
Bath

Cl.

Her Bath

Her
Dressing
Room

Open To
Below

Bedroom

His
Vest.

His Dressing
Room

Elev.

Bath

Cl.

W.C.

Master Bedroom

Bridge

Vest.

Her Study

Terrace

Terrace

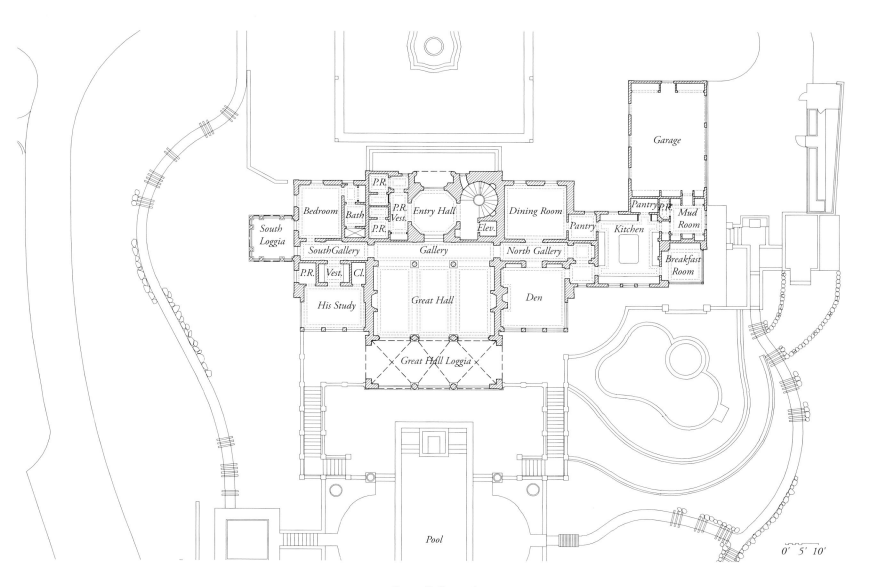

Garage

P.R.

P.R.
Vest.

Entry Hall

Dining Room

Pantry

Pantry

Mud
Room

Bedroom

Bath

P.R.

Elev.

Kitchen

South
Loggia

SouthGallery

Gallery

North Gallery

Breakfast
Room

P.R.

Vest.

Cl.

Great Hall

Den

His Study

Great Hall Loggia

Pool

0' 5' 10'

Ground floor plan

Watercolor study of the front facade

69

Watercolor study of the rear facade

1

2

3

4

Fig. 1: Detail from Casa de las Conchas, Salamanca, Spain, fifteenth century
Fig. 2: Window detail from Casa of Don Juan Marquez, Palma de Mallorca, Spain, seventeenth century
Fig. 3: Exterior of Weston Park, Staffordshire, England, 1760, James Paine *Fig. 4:* Sotto il Monte [La Toscana],
Santa Barbara, California, 1928, George Washington Smith *Fig. 5:* Detail of the side facade,
with a window and railing influenced by Spanish precedents [*p. 72, Fig. 2*] *Fig. 6:* Great room interior elevation:
progressive omission was used here, with the column bases removed to create a more rustic feel

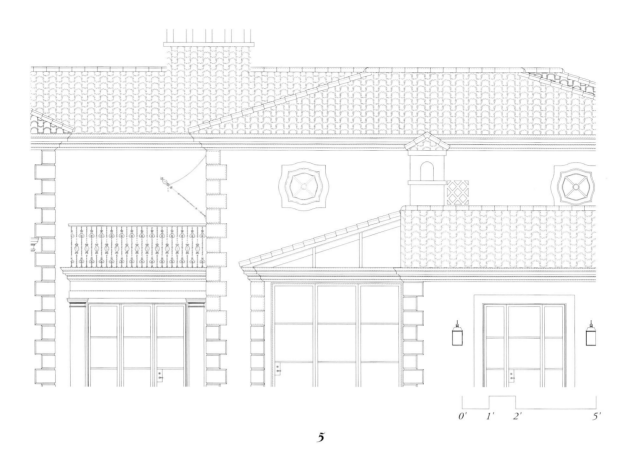

0' 1' 2'   5'

5

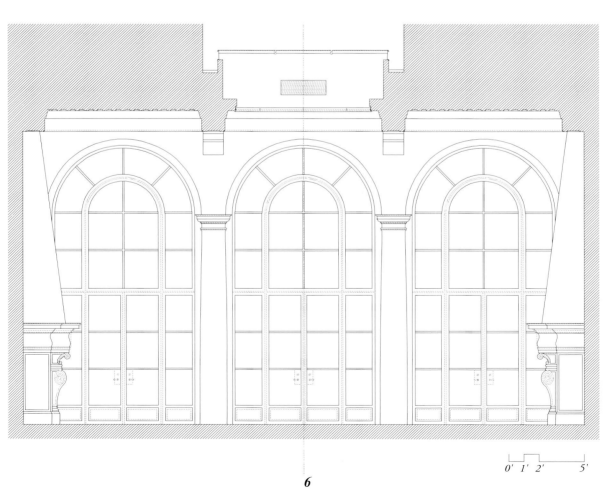

0' 1' 2'   5'

6

7

8

9

10

Fig. 7: Rear garden facade of the Kern House, Holmby Hills, California, 1925, George Washington Smith
Fig. 8: Pazo de Oca, Pontevedra, Galicia, Spain, 1783
Fig. 9: View of the guest house from the auto court *Fig. 10:* The groin vaults at the guest house loggia

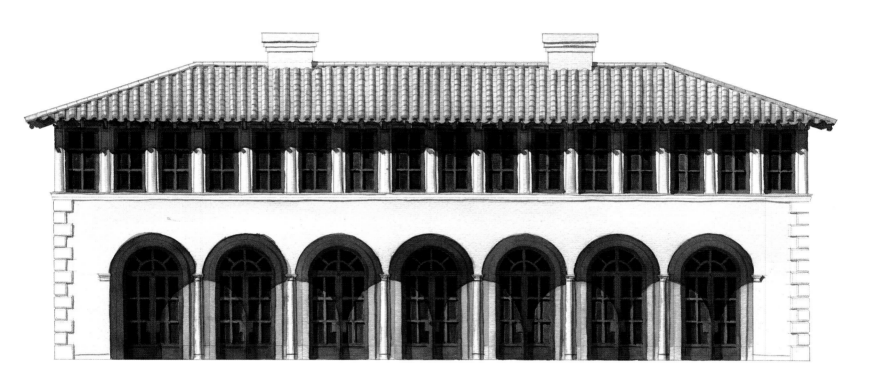

Watercolor study of the auto court office facade

THE RESORT AT PELICAN HILL

W OULD PALLADIO RECOGNIZE HIS DESCENDANTS? In this one-of-a-kind resort, designed for the Irvine Company, Palladian detailing and grand proportions abound. Yet if the size were reduced, and the palm trees replaced with umbrella pines and cypress trees, one would think it were sixteenth-century Italy with its symmetry, proportions, and forms that make up the design. The colors are Florentine: yellow ochre and gray pinks that perfectly complement the natural colors of California. The resort is all curves and domes. The main feature of the resort, the Coliseum, features a circular pool set within a curved colonnade and overlooks a tempietto that hosts weddings set against the Pacific Ocean [*p. 79; p. 88, Fig. 9*].

Irvine's chairman, Donald Bren, had become interested in Palladian architecture in the 1980s while on a trip to Italy and wanted a unique resort that would fit in with the Mediterranean architectural style of the Newport coast. Monumental in scale, it took a full team of architects and designers to complete this project. The interior architecture of the hotel, spa, villa clubhouse, golf clubhouse, coliseum, and wedding pavilion was our area of focus. The villa clubhouse itself is,

Left: Interior of La Rocca Pisana, Lonigo, Italy, 1576, Vincenzo Scamozzi
Opposite: The rotunda at the hotel lobby

essentially, an entirely separate hotel within the hotel. Found within a gated area of the resort, the clubhouse serves the surrounding villas with a bar, restaurant, fitness area, and concierge devoted solely to those guests [*p. 83*]. We only designed the interior architecture of the various buildings, but the work was not confined to an exterior given to us by another architect. Rather, we designed the plan so that it would function well and create exciting promenades, and worked with both the exterior architect and Darryl Schmidt, the interior designer, to shape it in such a way that the interior and exterior worked harmoniously.

The planning style for this project is typically Italian. Although the main source of inspiration was Palladio's symmetrical villas, the site was located on a steep slope, which required a different type of planning. To locate the buildings on the site, Robert Elliott, head of urban planning at Irvine, took an approach nearer to the organic layout of the Seven Hills in Rome. First, the topography determined the locations of buildings, then those areas were regularized into formal compositions. This organic urban scheme, combined with the formal ordering of Palladio, creates an interesting mix of axes and views as one walks about the resort.

The Doric order after de l'Orme and the base of the Tuscan order after Palladio were used to create the order predominant in the design [*p. 84, Figs. 4, 5*]. The Doric order is used to full effect in the lobby of the hotel, where it supports a 28-foot-tall dome with an oculus puncturing the center inspired by the Pantheon in Rome [*p. 77*]. A variation on this theme is used at the entrance hall rotunda of the spa, where pairs of Doric columns again support a rotunda, this time in the form of an octagon [*p. 86, Fig. 7*]. Small rotundas are found at each of the intersections of the various galleries to create the feeling of an ancient Roman bath. Inspired by the pool at the Ferncliff Casino (1904) in Rhinebeck, New York, by McKim, Mead & White, we created vaulted ceilings in the actual spa areas [*p. 80, Fig. 1*]. These cloudlike forms with their airy and serene atmosphere enhance the luxurious spa experience [*p. 81*].

Loggias are another trademark of Palladio. Both the Villa Barbaro (1560) at Maser and the Villa Emo (1559) at Treviso by Palladio have large, double-height loggias formed by piers for circulation and covered outdoor living space [*p. 84, Figs. 3, 6*]. Similar dining loggias were created for the hotel restaurant, Andrea [*p. 85*]. The loggia form was also used to create romantic covered walkways at the hotel and golf clubhouse. A colonnade with Doric columns was used at the rear of both the villa clubhouse to create a dining terrace and the main hotel to frame the magnificent view out over the golf course to the coast.

Opposite, above: Coliseum terrace *Opposite, below:* Coliseum floor plan

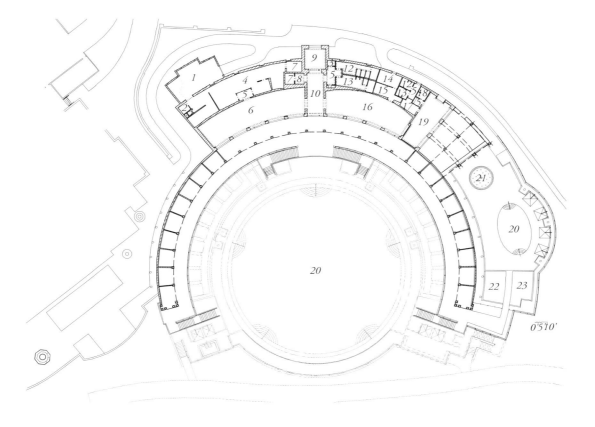

1. Service
2. Restroom
3. Janitor
4. Kitchen
5. Vestibule
6. Dining Room
7. Elevator
8. Elevator Vestibule
9. Tower
10. Gallery
11. Closet
12. Women's Restroom
13. Men's Restroom
14. Storage
15. Liquor Storage
16. Bar
17. Kitchen
18. Unisex Restroom
19. Kid's Club
20. Pool
21. Water Feature
22. Lawn
23. Sand Play Area

The Coliseum surrounding the 136-foot main pool of the resort is based on Palladian architecture and ancient amphitheatres [*p. 79*]. The enclosing arms of the coliseum step down through a series of terraces to the water, reminiscent of a semi-circular Greek theater, with a view out to the coast. The addition of a columnar portico based upon the curved portico at Palladio's Villa Badoer (1556) in Fratta Polesine, Italy, is a shaded escape from the sun for dining and unites the typically Greek, semi-circular theater form with an Italian colonnade to connect to the Italian style prevalent throughout the resort.

The wedding pavilion was based upon various garden follies, drawing a great deal from the Temple of Apollo (1776) at the Garden of Pan and Galatea in Schwetzingen, Germany, by Nicholas de Pigage [*p. 88, Fig. 10*]. A circular tholos was created out of Doric columns supporting a full entablature and dome, clad in custom clay fishscale roof tiles above [*p. 89*]. Located at the edge of an oval-shaped lawn, the folly accentuates the view of the ocean beyond with a point of interest and creates a romantic air [*p. 88, Fig. 9*]. The frieze of the entablature is simplified; the trigylph becomes the flat field while the metopes are recessed. The metopes were handmade of terra-cotta and punctuate the horizontal band to bring interest to the composition.

Fig. 1: Pool at the Ferncliff Casino, Rhinebeck, New York, 1904, McKim, Mead & White
Fig. 2: Cafe display case from the Cafe Pushkin, Moscow, Russia, 1999, Andrei Dellos
Opposite, above: Interior of the spa

1

2

Opposite, below: The octagonal cafe required a large bar to display food, which had to be resolved within the form. Various bars and display cases in European cafes were looked at for precedents [*above, Fig. 2*]. Ultimately, the geometric form was complemented by a segmented bar that protrudes into the space, reflecting the angles of the interior walls.

Above: Rotunda at the hotel lobby reception area *Below:* The Andrea Restaurant

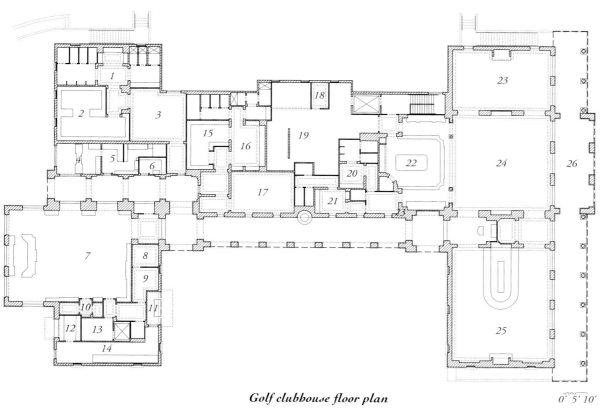

Golf clubhouse floor plan

0' 5' 10'

1. Men's Restroom
2. Men's Lockers
3. Men's Lounge
4. Coffee Bar
5. Coffee Bar Storage
6. Shoe Attendant
7. Golf Shop
8. Golf General Manager
9. Assistant
10. Dressing Rooms
11. Valet
12. Ball Attendant
13. Golf Shop Storage
14. Ball Storage
15. Women's Lockers
16. Women's Restroom
17. Women's Lounge
18. Office
19. Kitchen
20. Men's Restroom
21. Women's Restroom
22. Disply Kitchen
23. Private Dining
24. Dining Room
25. Bar/Lounge
26. Terrace

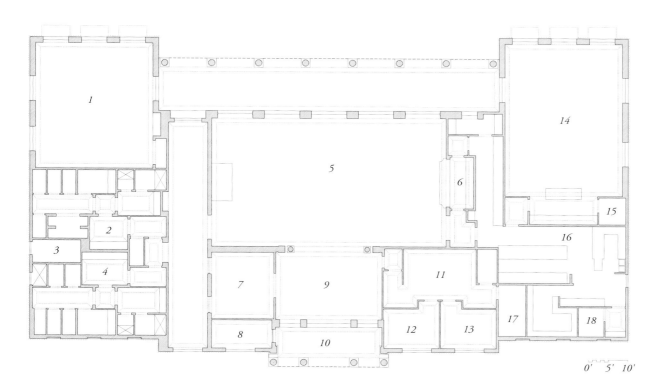

1. Fitness Room
2. Men's Restroom
3. Electrical
4. Women's Restroom
5. Great Room
6. Bar
7. Concierge
8. Valet
9. Lobby
10. Exterior Porch
11. Adminstration
12. Adminstration Assistant
13. General Manager
14. Dining
15. Storage
16. Kitchen
17. Storage
18. Restroom

0' 5' 10'

Villa clubhouse floor plan

3

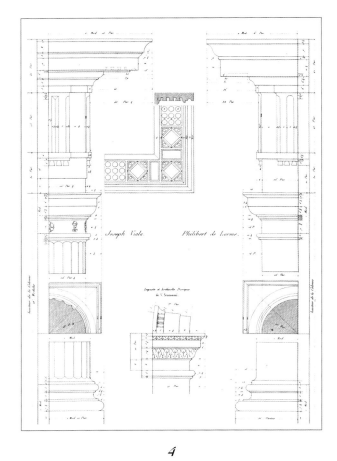

4

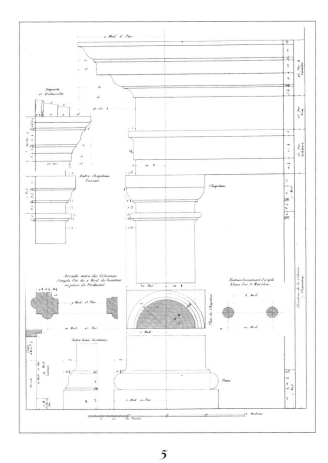

5

6

Fig. 3: Villa Emo, Treviso, Italy, 1559, Andrea Palladio *Fig. 4:* Doric order after Zanini and de l'Orme
Fig. 5: Tuscan order after Palladio *Fig. 6:* Villa Barbaro, Maser, Italy, 1560, Andrea Palladio
Opposite, above: View of the coast from the loggia *Opposite, below:* View of the dining terrace at Andrea

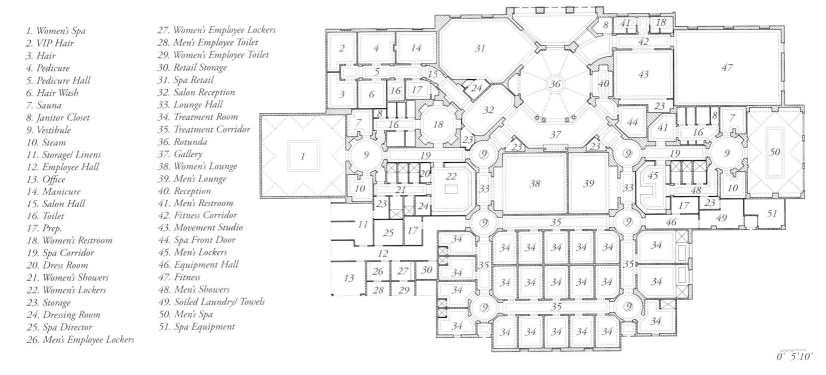

1. Women's Spa
2. VIP Hair
3. Hair
4. Pedicure
5. Pedicure Hall
6. Hair Wash
7. Sauna
8. Janitor Closet
9. Vestibule
10. Steam
11. Storage/ Linens
12. Employee Hall
13. Office
14. Manicure
15. Salon Hall
16. Toilet
17. Prep.
18. Women's Restroom
19. Spa Corridor
20. Dress Room
21. Women's Showers
22. Women's Lockers
23. Storage
24. Dressing Room
25. Spa Director
26. Men's Employee Lockers
27. Women's Employee Lockers
28. Men's Employee Toilet
29. Women's Employee Toilet
30. Retail Storage
31. Spa Retail
32. Salon Reception
33. Lounge Hall
34. Treatment Room
35. Treatment Corridor
36. Rotunda
37. Gallery
38. Women's Lounge
39. Men's Lounge
40. Reception
41. Men's Restroom
42. Fitness Corridor
43. Movement Studio
44. Spa Front Door
45. Men's Lockers
46. Equipment Hall
47. Fitness
48. Men's Showers
49. Soiled Laundry/ Towels
50. Men's Spa
51. Spa Equipment

0' 5'10'

Spa floor plan

7

8

Fig. 7: The spa lobby with an octagonal dome above ***Fig. 8:*** The bar at the golf clubhouse
Opposite: The great room at the villa clubhouse

86

9

Fig. 9: Wedding pavilion
with an oval terrace
Fig. 10: Temple of Apollo
at the Garden of Pan and
Galatea, Schwetzingen,
Baden-Wurttemberg, 1776,
Nicholas de Pigage
Opposite: Watercolor study
of the pavilion

10

89

FRENCH ARCHITECTURE

The range and wealth of French architectural styles is enormous, as befits a country that extends from the cold northern Atlantic to the warm shores of the Mediterranean. In the sixteenth century, the architectural gap between the end of the Medieval era and the start of the French Renaissance (about 1495) was bridged by the châteaux of the Loire Valley. Medieval forms ornamented with classical detailing such as Chambord, with round towers typical of a castle, and Chenonceau, with its picturesque arches and turrets rising from the water, are two fine examples.

The design for Vaux le Vicomte, for instance, is so astounding that even King Louis XIV was jealous of owner Nicolas Fouquet. After throwing him in jail under suspicion of embezzlement, the king used Fouquet's architects, Louis Le Vau and Charles Le Brun, to build Versailles amid exquisite formal gardens designed by André Le Nôtre. Versailles is a wondrous place that exhibits all the crowning achievements of the seventeenth century in the main buildings of the palace, and in sublime outlying pavilions like the Petit Trianon and others of the eighteenth century, added later by Louis XV and Louis XVI.

The nineteenth century brought an increased interest in antiquity with the advent of new archaeological discoveries and Napoleon's conquest of Egypt, a great example of which is Percier and Fontaine's Malmaison.

A FRENCH COUNTRY HOUSE

I THINK OF THIS HOUSE AS THE ULTIMATE FAMILY home. The dining room is made for family gatherings, with a large, welcoming table and green floral walls that open out to the garden. Green on green, this room is a place for memories par excellence. The layout of the plan is similar to John Russell Pope's unbuilt project for Prince Christopher of Greece, to have been between 96th and 97th streets in New York [*p. 94*]. In that plan, Pope gave the most important rooms views of Fifth Avenue and placed the entrance on an alley between Fifth and Madison. In this design, the dining room along with the living and family rooms have the best views of the rear gardens to allow for easy access to nature for the children [*p. 95*]. The main entry, stair hall, and gallery are all on an axis with the dining room. This impressive enfilade flows to a spectacular view of the garden from the dining room, creating a feeling of movement through the house.

The main entry is the focal point of a strongly symmetrical composition with a broken triangular pediment that signals the entry point [*pp. 93, 97*]. Four Tuscan columns in a larger central bay support a coffered barrel vault—reminiscent of the Doric portico of Palladio's Basilica in Vicenza—that fits a double-height arched door made in France [*p. 96, Fig. 1*]. A small circular window within the over-door panel lines up with the balustrade pattern set into the wainscoting of the interior stair hall. This gives a glimpse of the Diane Chapman–designed interior spaces [*p. 105*]. A lantern completes the composition, attached to the coffers by four chains to prevent it from hitting the house in a strong wind.

Upon entering the vestibule, there appears to be only one path through to the stair hall, but there are actually two hidden studies to the left and right, accessible through blind doors in the paneling. Moving through the vestibule, one enters the stair hall. The staircase wraps around the hall as it rises, becoming a gallery space above that is set back from the walls of the lower hall. Coupled with a large lay light, this creates a space that opens dramatically as it is walked through. The stair hall at the

Opposite: Front entry

seventeenth-century Hotel Aubert de Fontenay in Paris by Jean Boullier de Bourges, now the Picasso Museum, served as inspiration for this dynamic space [*p. 104, Fig. 16*].

After passing through the stair hall and gallery, one reaches the racetrack-shaped dining room. The dining room is also accessible from a side door to the living room, allowing for easy circulation during events such as a buffet dinner [*p. 106, Fig. 19; p. 107*]. Inspired by John Russell Pope's Laughlin House (1922), the dining room projects from the rear facade as a half-circular volume [*p. 96, Fig. 5*]. Three pairs of arched French doors provide a spectacular view into the gardens. A pair of Tuscan columns based on Serlio's order flank the sides of each door. A pilaster takes the place of the column where the circular form meets the rectilinear main portion of the house. These columns support a full entablature with a terrace above that serves the study, itself set slightly forward from the plane of the house [*p. 98, Fig. 13*]. To enhance the sculptural quality of this volume sweeping out from the planar elevation, the columns are pulled slightly out from the circular wall. This leads to a feeling of tension between the volume of the dining room and the columnar screen [*p. 99*].

The symmetry of the rear elevation is further enhanced by utilizing a lesson learned from two seventeenth-century houses in Versailles [*p. 96, Figs. 3 and 4*]. The two side terraces that bookend the rear facade are set back from the face of it the distance of the quoining. The central portion of the rear elevation is topped by a curved pediment similar to that found at L'Ermitage de Madame Pompadour (1747) in Fontainebleau, France [*p. 96, Fig. 2*]. Coupled with the curved terrace extending before it, this creates a unique composition of curves on two planes of the house and breaks the facade into separate volumes, creating a distinct hierarchy of the spaces represented behind the elevation [*pp. 102–03*].

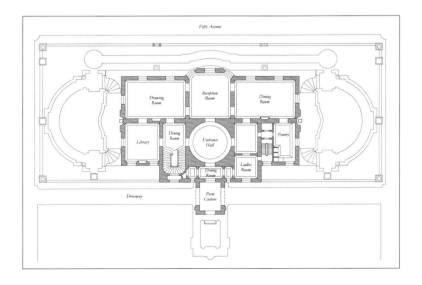

Plan of an unbuilt residence for Prince Christopher of Greece, Fifth Avenue between 96th and 97th Street, New York, 1915, John Russell Pope

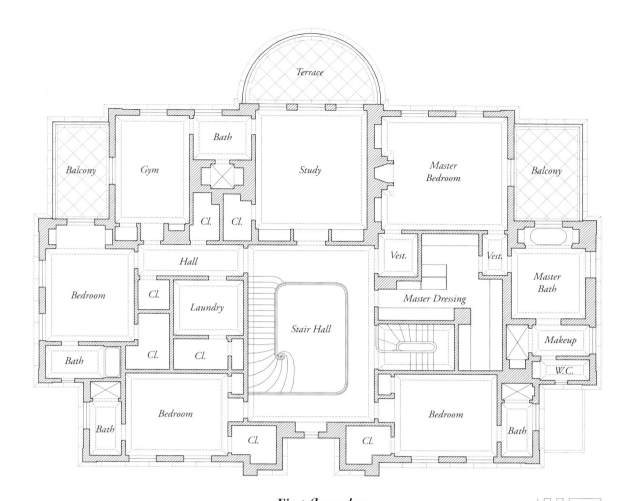

First floor plan

0' 5' 10'

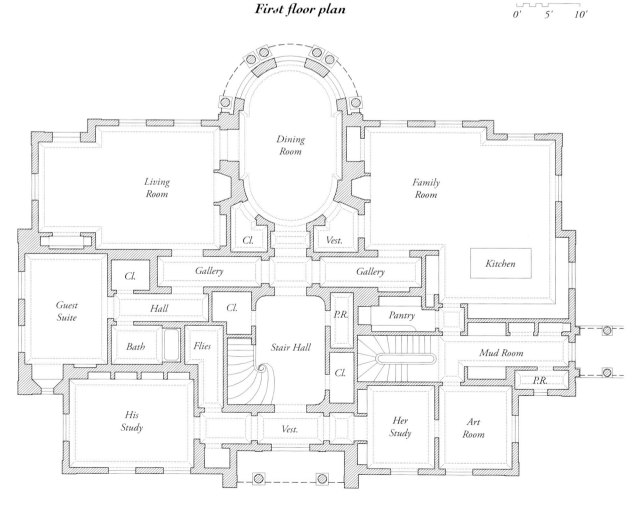

Ground floor plan

0' 5' 10'

1

2

3

4

5

Fig. 1: Doric portico of the Basilica Palladiana, Vicenza, 1614, Andrea Palladio *Fig. 2:* L'Ermitage de Madame Pompadour, Fontainebleau, France, 1747, Jacques-Ange Gabriel *Fig. 3:* Hôtel de la Chancellerie, Versailles, 1672, François d'Orbay *Fig. 4:* 93 Rue Royale, Versailles, eighteenth century *Fig.5:* Laughlin House, Meridian Hill, Washington, DC, 1922, John Russell Pope

96

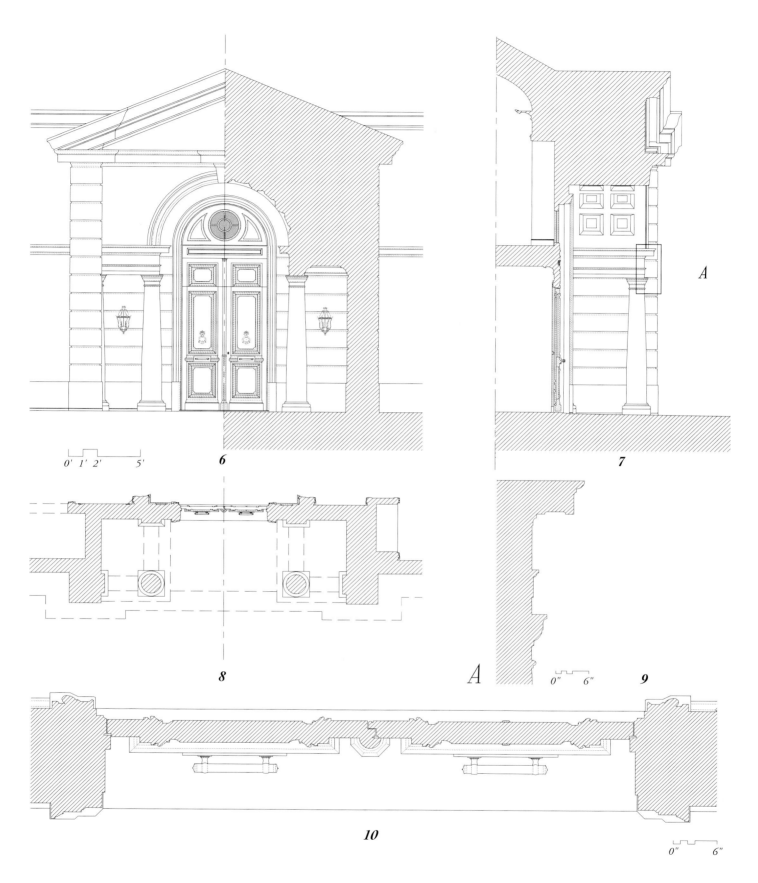

0' 1' 2'   5'   **6**   **7**

8   *A*   0"   6"   **9**

10   0"   6"

Fig. 6: Elevation of the front entry ***Fig. 7:*** Section of the front entry ***Fig. 8:*** Plan of the front entry
Fig. 9: Entablature detail of the front entry ***Fig. 10:*** Detail plan of the front entry door. This was inspired by a nineteenth-century Parisian entrance door [*p. 104, Fig. 15*].

11

12

13

Fig. 11: Approach to the front entry ***Fig. 12:*** Side view ***Fig. 13:*** Rear garden elevation
Opposite: Detail of rear garden elevation

Watercolor study of the front facade

Watercolor study of the garden facade

14

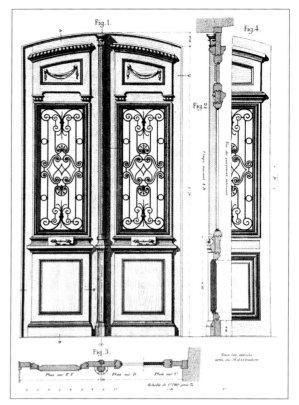

15

16

17

18

Fig. 14. Laurentian Library, Florence, sixteenth century, Michelangelo *Fig. 15:* Detail of nineteenth-century Parisian entrance doors *Fig. 16:* Hotel Aubert de Fontenay, Rue de Thorigny in the Marais, 1660, Jean Boullier de Bourges *Fig. 17:* Ornamental wrought iron newel post at 17 Rue Guénégaud, Paris 6th, 1665 *Fig. 18:* Railing at 27 Rue Danielle Casanova, Paris 1st, 1707

View of the stair hall. A paving pattern of French limestone and Belgian black marble cabochons unifies the various rooms of the house. An integral part of the plan, the pattern aligns with the various rooms it is located in, flowing seamlessly through the house. The stone was honed in place, creating a surface that feels lived in. The stair curls back in on itself in plan as it reaches the ground floor, a detail inspired by the stair at 17 Rue Guénégaud [*p. 104, Fig. 17*]. The balustrade is made of wrought iron painted satin black with gold leaf accents, with a design similar to the historical precedent found at 17 Rue Danielle-Casanova [*p. 104, Fig. 18*]. The stair treads are limestone, while the curved risers are of fausse pierre (faux stone). A brass lantern hangs from the lay light above. At the top of the photo behind the balustrade, the circular window in the over door of the entrance provides a view of the entry drive.

19

20

21

Fig. 19: View from the living room to the dining

Fig. 20: Master bathroom, with an oval step inspired by the stair at the Laurentian Library [*p. 104, Fig. 14*]

Fig. 21: Kitchen, fabricated from bleached rift-sawn white oak, with honed Calacatta marble counters and splash

Opposite: View through French doors from the gallery to the dining room and garden beyond

A CITY APARTMENT

THIS APARTMENT IS AN ODE TO FRENCH CLASSICISM. Located in a 1914 Beaux-Arts building with a curvaceous exterior facade, the use of ovals and circles as a recurring motif in the interior architecture was an obvious choice. With the support of our client, the apartment was gutted to allow complete flexibility in the new design. We then implemented a typically French interior with Louis XVI paneling, Louis XV furniture, and moldings inspired by those at the Château de Villette (1668) by J. H. Mansard in Meulan, France. In this San Franciscan apartment, floor patterns were designed for each room, and the parquet de Versailles, chevron patterns, and radial chevrons were painstakingly distressed to look old.

A curvilinear gallery was created around the stair hall as the primary circulation device other than the enfilade circulation between the public rooms [*p. 112*]. The entrance hall, located off of the gallery, is circular in shape and leads into the living room [*p. 109*]. Everything in this room reflects the curved exterior of the building, right down to its floor pattern. This is articulated with a dark brown marble border surrounding a field marked by circular cabochons.

The master bedroom is accessed off of the gallery while the bath and his and her dressing rooms are found off of a vestibule within [*p. 115*]. The master bath is located adjacent to a curved exterior wall. The curve of the exterior wall was mirrored to create a tonneau, or barrel-shaped room; creating rooms from geometric forms other than squares or rectangles is a typically French notion. The racetrack-shaped tub has a pattern of brown marble surrounding it and sits centered in this dramatic space [*p. 114*].

The dining room is an expression of pure form: a circle with flat, recessed niches set into the paneling allows gilded consoles with mirrors above [*p. 113*]. The client, a redhead with a very light complexion, asked interior designer Suzanne Tucker to choose a color scheme that would complement her looks.

Opposite: View from the gallery of the entrance hall

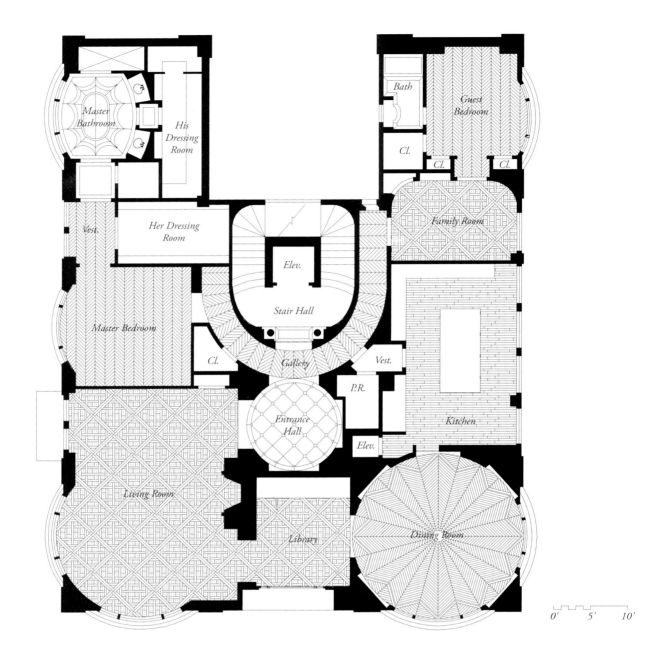

The dining room captures this with a radial chevron white oak floor, dark-paneled walls finished in a bittersweet chocolate color, and a burnished gold-leaf ceiling with a raised circular panel at the center of the ceiling. This raised panel utilizes uplighting to add warmth and drama to the space. From the center of this circular panel, a chandelier is attached to a small motor, allowing it to be lowered or raised and the hostess to light the candles she puts into it before each dinner party as a throwback to earlier times. Large windows provide views out over the city from wrought-iron balconies, creating a dining room that is rich in both its colors and reflectivity while remaining open to the spectacular views afforded by its location.

Above: Apartment floor plan *Opposite:* The white oak paneled library

Above: View of the entrance hall and living room beyond from the gallery ***Opposite:*** Dining room

1

2

3

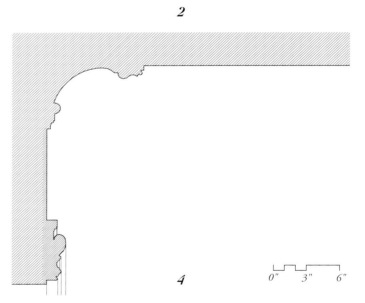

4

0"   3"   6"

Fig. 1: Enfilade entry to the master bath from the master bedroom
Fig. 2: The master bath
Fig. 3: Curved vanity detail
Fig. 4: Detail of the crown molding and casing
Opposite: Master bedroom with a curved bay window

A FRENCH RENAISSANCE HOUSE
Under Construction

Enamored with the Renaissance châteaux of the Loire Valley, the clients wished to build this house, their main residence, in the French Renaissance style. Two of my favorite châteaux came to inspire the residence. As in the Château de Chambord (1547) in Loir-et-Cher, France, I placed two half towers on the front facade at a distance from the corners [*p. 119, Fig. 4*]. Drawing upon the sixteenth-century Château de Valençay in Berry as another precedent, the towers have hemispherical domes typical to the Renaissance [*p. 118, Fig. 1*]. Three arched bays make up the center of the facade, with Corinthian columns on the ground floor supporting Composite columns on the first floor in a manner seen at Chambord. The front entrance is marked by a triangular pediment supported by two levels of columns, creating a rigorously symmetrical entrance facade which any king or prince of France would feel at home with [*pp. 120–21*].

Many of the buildings used for precedent were located in northern France, but this building needed to respond to a more temperate climate. To do so, the château was theoretically placed in southern France. Imagining it in this area, we were inspired by Romanesque and Cistercian abbeys for the materials and colors. The Sénanque Abbey (1178) in Gordes, France, offered a warm color palette of stone and earth-fired clay roof tiles. The house has a large loggia centered on the rear elevation, located off the family room [*p. 117; p. 119*]. This creates a large, covered outdoor living area for the family to enjoy. Because the loggia otherwise plunges the family room into shadow, a large skylight on the roof brings in natural light through a large lay light.

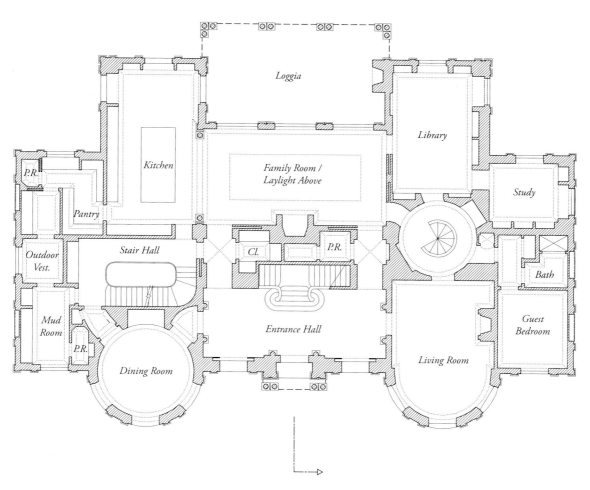

Ground floor plan

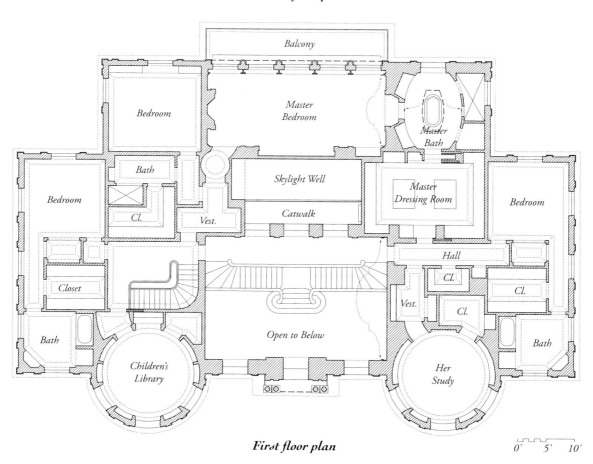

First floor plan

0' 5' 10'

For the rear facade design, the Villa Garzoni (1539) in Pontecasale, Italy, by Cesare Gerolimetto served as inspiration [*p. 118, Fig. 2*]. This villa has a similar ordering system in the facade: two levels of columns frame arches for an open loggia in the middle with solid towers on the sides. This became the basis for the design of the garden facade. The central portion is open on the ground floor for the loggia and solid side portions create a tripartite facade.

The plan for this residence is based around the central entrance hall and family room, with interior design by Karen Yttrup, which are connected by sliding doors. The entrance stair is similar to Pierre Contant d'Ivry's Grand Escalier of the Palais-Royal in Paris (1768) [*p. 119, Fig. 3*]. The family room lies opposite the stair. These two spaces mediate between the two sides of the ground floor, one containing the dining room and kitchen, the other the library and living room. Above, the first floor contains the family's bedrooms. The master bedroom is placed in the center, with a balcony looking out over the gardens, while the children's bedrooms surround it, offering close proximity and views to the rear garden. On this level, the two turrets become a children's library and office, creating private spaces with 180-degree views of the front drive and gardens.

Fig. 1: Château de Valençay, Berry, France, eighteenth century
Fig. 2: Villa Garzoni, Pontecasale, Italy, 1539, Cesare Gerolimetto

1

2

Light Well

Master Bedroom

Laylight

Entrance Hall

Loggia

Family Room

P.R.

Theatre

Vest.

Hall

Mechanical Room

Longitudinal section

0'   5'   10'

3

4

Fig. 3: Grand Escalier of the Palais-Royal, Paris, France, 1768, Pierre Contant d'Ivry
Fig. 4: Château de Chambord, Chambord, Loir-et-Cher, France, 1547

Watercolor study of the front facade

A COUNTRY RESIDENCE

THIS HOUSE, WHOSE STRAIGHT LINES AND DETAILS relate perfectly to the whole, has a simple elegance that is rarely achieved, and is to me, La Crèmerie. The parents of a previous client came to me to design a modest yet elegant house in the French style. After meeting in our library, they chose two of the smaller buildings in Versailles to serve as my inspiration. In response, I gave them this house, a place that but for skies a bit more gray and less blue, would be perfectly at home in the Ile-de-France, built during the Ancien Regime.

Desiring an easily livable house, the couple asked for all the major spaces of the house on one level [*p. 125*]. In order to give the facade the necessary proportions of a typical French house, a large mansard roof with segmental arched dormers was added based on the mid-eighteenth century l'Aile des Ecuries in France by Jacques-François Blondel [*p. 124, Fig. 2*]. This not only succeeded in solving the issues inherent in a one-story elevation, but allowed for great freedom in sculpting the interior volumes. I was able to vary the ceiling heights and create lay lights wherever I wanted without worrying about rooms above.

The house was laid out in a U shape to allow natural lighting in all the rooms, with interior design by Steven Volpe Design [*p. 124, Fig. 1*]. This works especially well in the master bedroom and his study, as light enters these rooms from two and three sides respectively. Creating a building of this (or some other) shape only one room deep is one of my favorite things to do, as it allows lots of natural light into all the rooms of a house. Enfilade circulation between rooms becomes a necessity, which greatly adds to the excitement one feels walking through the house.

The center section of the house is devoted to the public spaces and contains an entrance hall with a large lay light above that opens on axis to the great hall and two galleries on the perpendicular axis [*p. 130*]. The great hall has a 13-foot-tall ceiling to create a spacious, well-proportioned room. A fireplace is located on the side wall of the great hall and lines up with an antique armoire that hides the bar within it [*p. 131*]. Four circular, domed vestibules act as hinges to mediate between the orthogonal geometry of the main house and the octagonal spaces adjacent to them [*p. 129*].

Opposite: Rear elevation

1

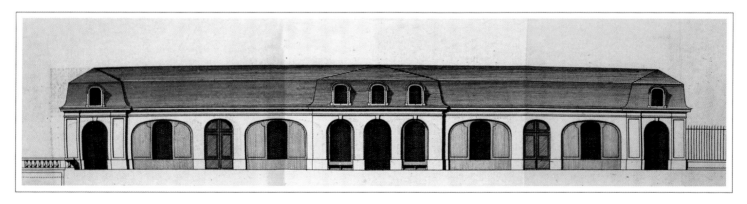

2

Fig. 1: Front elevation *Fig. 2:* L'Aile des Ecuries, France, 1730s, Jacques-François Blondel

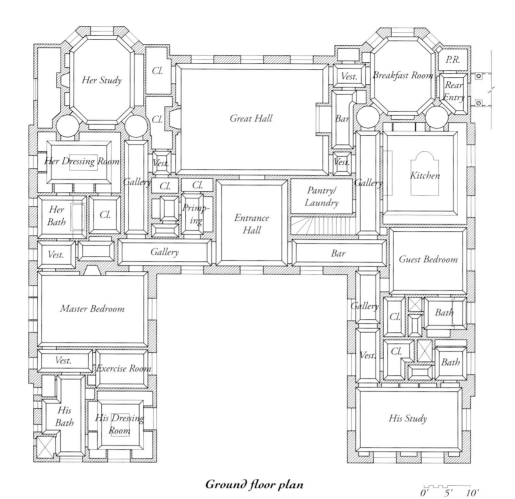

Ground floor plan

0' 5' 10'

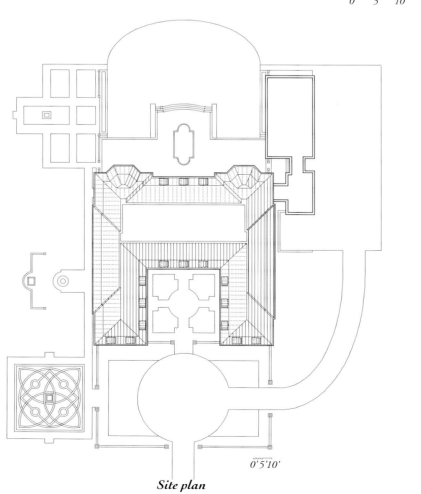

Site plan

0' 5' 10'

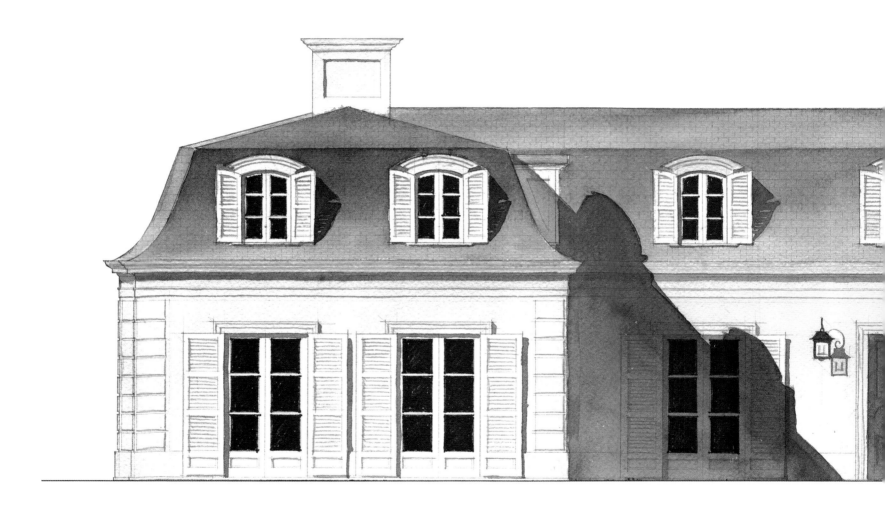

Watercolor study of the front facade

3

4

5

Fig. 3: Her study
Fig. 4: Stair at the Hôtel le Lièvre de la Grange, Paris, France, 1737, Theirry-Victor Dailley
Fig. 5: Detail of the wainscoting termination
Opposite: One of the four circular "hinge" vestibules. These domed spaces mediate between the orthogonal geometry of the main house and the octagonal geometry of her study and the breakfast room. They also create a moment of repose at the end of the two galleries before entering the spaces.

Above: View of the entrance hall and lay light
Opposite: The fireplace in the great hall

A TOWNHOUSE

AN ELABORATE BRONZE AND GLASS MARQUISE over the entrance welcomes visitors to this townhouse. The clients wanted an entry that would make a statement about their newly renovated residence, and the strong French architecture does just that. To design this undeniably French fan-shaped canopy, I drew from my memories of walks through Paris with my wife Françoise [*p. 133*]. Large French entry doors allow a glimpse of the front hall interior and draw visitors into the space. Paneling with curvaceous Louis XV profiles break up the large surfaces of the interior walls in a simple Louis XVI manner, and a wrought-iron balustrade in the Louis XV style is capped with a polished bronze rail [*p. 135*]. The richness of this composition is enhanced by the diamond-patterned limestone and white oak flooring which creates an entry sequence befitting this grand townhouse [*p. 134*].

This renovation began with gutting the existing townhouse, even replacing the existing windows with casement windows to give it a French character. The plan was reconfigured, the separate garage demolished, and an integral garage was built. The new garage allows direct access from the basement via a curved stair, now housed within a bay window—something the clients insisted upon in the design [*p. 137*]. The basement in the existing house was small and cramped, with low ceilings that extended underneath only part of the house. After gutting the interior, a proper basement was excavated to create a fantastic guest suite on that level.

As a modified French style residence, the existing house had a steeply pitched roofline with an unfinished attic—an egregious waste of livable space. The space was re-designed as a series of two guest suites and his impressive study, with interior design by Suzanne Tucker [*p. 136; p. 141*]. New dormer windows were added to bring light and air into these rooms, giving them the feel of being within a mansard roof [*p. 140, Figs. 4 and 5*]. Another distinctive element of this house is the dining room. The architectural decoration is simple, serving as a frame for a beautiful mural painted by Willem Racké, which depicts the view out over the water to the opposite shore from the site [*p. 138*].

Opposite: Entrance

1

2

3

Figs. 1–3, and opposite: Views of the entrance hall

134

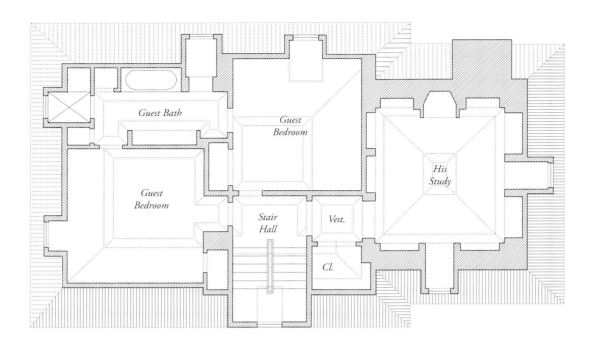

Attic floor plan

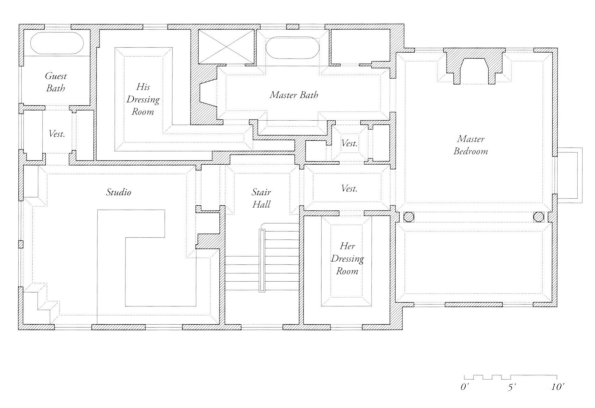

0'   5'   10'

First floor plan

136

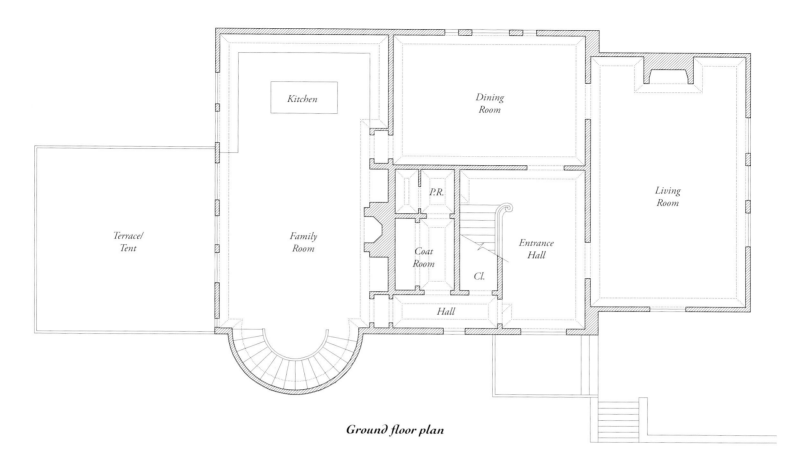

Ground floor plan

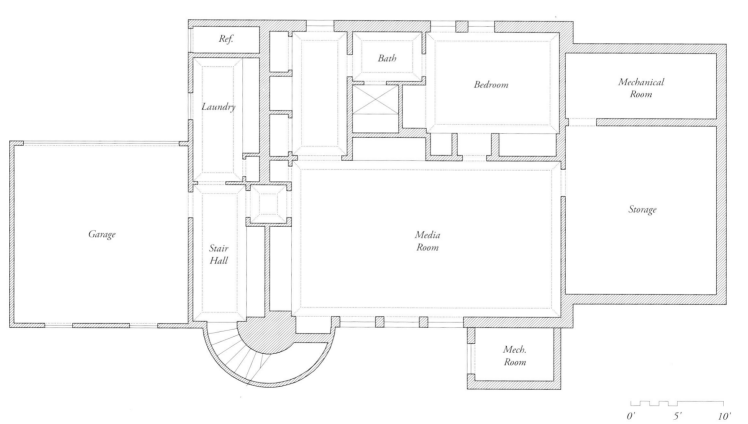

Basement floor plan

137

Above: Living room *Below:* Dining room *Opposite:* Detail of the paneling in the living room

4

5

6

Fig. 4: Dormer window
in a guest bedroom
Fig. 5: Guest bedroom
inside the mansard roof
Fig. 6: Interior of the
dining tent
Opposite: His study

A CITY APARTMENT
IN THE HAUSSMANNIAN STYLE

O NE OF THE JOYS OF DESIGNING DOMESTIC
architecture is having the ability to give people a specific program that fits their personal lifestyle. This apartment, located in a Beaux-Arts apartment building, has views of a park in front, the water to the rear, and a landscaped courtyard with gardens at one side. The full-floor apartment was completely gutted and put back together in such a way that it perfectly matched the clients' personal needs and tastes.

The most remarkable programmatic requirement in this design was the huge, contiguous master suite [*p. 144*]. Both the husband and wife wanted their own respective baths, dressing rooms, and offices located directly off of the master bedroom. They also wanted an attached exercise room. The clients enjoy selecting their clothes and wanted them displayed as in a boutique. In his dressing room, the ties take center stage on a magnificent tie rack where they are color coded and displayed adjacent to his coat rack [*p. 152, Figs. 4, 6*]. In his oak-paneled bathroom, large mirrors, a polished nickel and etched starfire glass shower, and exquisite crown moldings complete a room that celebrates the acts of dressing and choosing one's clothes for the day [*p. 152, Fig. 7*]. Her dressing room is really a sitting room, with a chaise lounge and mirrored, paneled closet doors that fold into three-way mirrors [*p. 153*].

The other rooms of the apartment, with interior design by Suzanne Tucker, match the level of luxury found within the master suite. The paneled entrance hall is oval in shape, and has a lantern at the center hanging from an up-lit recessed panel in the ceiling and an elaborate floor pattern [*p. 143*]. A long gallery leads to the master suite while the other rooms are found off of the other three axial openings [*p. 149*]. The library, located on the cross-axis, is detailed in walnut paneling [*p. 150; p. 151*]. Opposite the gallery are the living and dining rooms where fluted pilasters in the Doric order regularize and add detail [*p. 145*]. These same pilasters are used throughout the apartment to form, for example, the elaborate door surrounds that frame the fireplace, the entrance to each room, and

Opposite: View of the entrance hall from the living room

142

windows to the exterior [*p. 150*]. Two columns frame the view from the living room out through the alcove to the water beyond, creating a particularly powerful view [*pp. 146–47*]. Since the clients wanted high doors and openings that matched the height of the exterior openings, the entablature above the columns and pilasters has been suppressed. The compressed entablatures with French-style crowns give the spaces a Haussmannian feel.

The kitchen was another interesting aspect of this design. An air shaft running through the entire apartment and the need for regularized spaces for the other rooms required the kitchen to take an inverted U-shaped form with an attached arm at the top [*p. 144; p. 148, Fig. 1*]. To allow room for storage in this tight space, the cabinetry was designed so that the doors would slide as opposed to swinging outward [*p. 148, Fig. 3*]. This was inspired by the floor to ceiling cupboards at the Butler's Pantry of the Biltmore Estate (1895) in Asheville, North Carolina, designed by Richard Morris Hunt [*p. 148, Fig. 2*]. This design not only saves space, but also allows the display of dinnerware. In my personal view, it is the future of contemporary kitchen design.

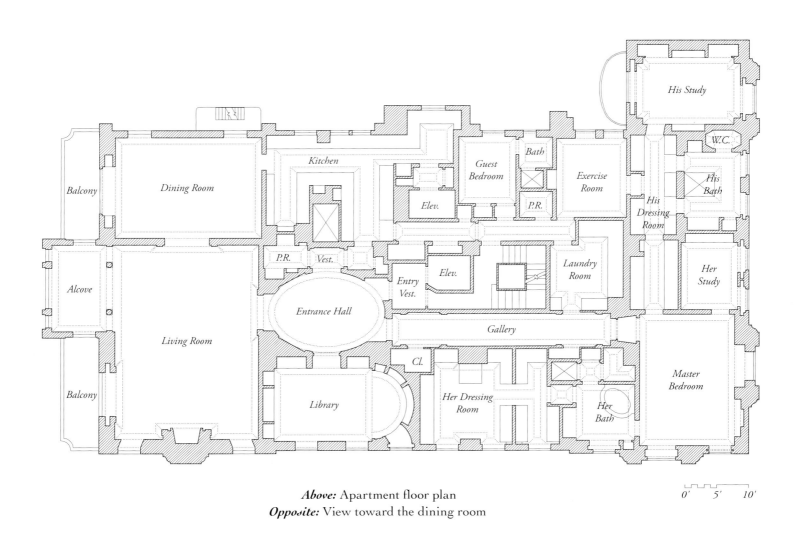

Above: Apartment floor plan
Opposite: View toward the dining room

Living room alcove

1

2

3

Fig. 1: Kitchen *Fig. 2:* Floor to ceiling cupboards at the Butler's Pantry of the Biltmore Estate, Asheville, North Carolina, 1895, Richard Morris Hunt *Fig. 3:* Sliding door cupboards in the kitchen *Opposite:* View down the gallery to the master bedroom

Above: Library *Below:* Living room *Opposite:* Detail of the curved wall at the end of the library

Fig. 4: His dressing room *Fig. 5:* Her bath *Fig. 6:* Tie rack in his dressing room
Fig. 7: His bath *Opposite:* Her dressing room

A NORMAN CARRIAGE HOUSE

EVERY INCH OF THIS CARRIAGE HOUSE WAS carefully designed to create an atmosphere that is rustic but also incredibly chic. The half-timbered walls and pyramidal roofs recall the architecture found on the western coast of France. This house could easily sit somewhere in Normandy. All the wooden elements are of Eastern white cedar, stained gray to create a delicately aged look. The client, a Francophile, requested that every detail be based on traditional vernacular French designs. The dormers, hinges, and outriggers on both the carriage house and the trellis are based on such precedents [*p. 154, Figs. 1 and 2*].

The carriage house was built on an existing estate with a working vineyard. This serene atmosphere transports visitors to some romantic locale in France. However, as a working farm, there was an unsightly water tower that fed the vines. The tower was incorporated into the new structure in the form of the octagonal tower that serves as a vertical element in the composition [*p. 155*]. A room was added above the actual tower and topped with an octagonal-pyramid roof clad in white cedar shingles. The form was derived from the dovecotes that dot the French countryside. Often circular or octagonal in shape, these medieval structures were often converted into homes, providing the perfect precedent for this tower.

Fig. 1: Langle, Doigt Valley, Normandy, France, late fifteenth century, La Rivière family
Fig. 2: La Pipardière, Pays d'Auge, Normandy, France, 1507, son of Jean de la Haye
Opposite, above: View of the carriage house from the drive through the working vineyard
Opposite, below: The carriage house doors and octagonal tower
Following page: Trellis at the main house

1

2

ALL PHOTOS THIS SECTION © STEVEN BROOKS STUDIO

A PALLADIAN ESTATE
Under Construction

COLOSSAL COLUMNS, MASSIVE SERLIAN windows, high walls of red brick with limestone accents, and a scale reminiscent of Versailles create quite the first impression [*p. 160, Fig. 2; pp. 162–63*]. It is very exciting to be approached to design a house as large as this one. The client for this project wanted a Palladian villa, with all the symmetry and grandeur accompanying that typology. Although many of Palladio's villas served as inspiration for this project, his Loggia del Capitaniato (1572) in Vicenza became the major driving force behind the detailing of the facade as it closely matched the project's scale [*p. 161*].

The large residential projects of McKim, Mead & White, such as the Frederick William Vanderbilt House (1899) in Hyde Park, New York, also helped with the overall massing of the villa and use of the colossal Corinthian order [*p. 160, Fig. 3*]. The client had desired a large porte-cochère, and that firm's Ogden Mills House (1897) in Staatsburg, New York, was a perfect example [*p. 160, Fig. 1*]. Here, the villa utilizes giant engaged pilasters, pulled in front of the house in the form of columns, to create a massive, pedimented porte-cochère.

The Loggia del Capitaniato's typical bay is formed of arched windows on the ground floor, rectangular windows on the first floor, and colossal engaged Corinthian columns [*p. 161*]. In this design, the columns were changed to pilasters in some areas and the bay was applied throughout. For the entry and sidewings, another motif from Palladio, the Serlian window that he had popularized, was used to punctuate three areas of the facade [*p. 159*].

Though the clients wanted a Palladian villa, a limestone and plaster facade would have been too bright and reflective for the local climatic conditions. The contrasting limestone columns and red brick of both Versailles and the Loggia del Capitaniato struck my clients. This allowed a more subdued color scheme: the brick will absorb much of the light while the stone accents will provide the richness of material and detail.

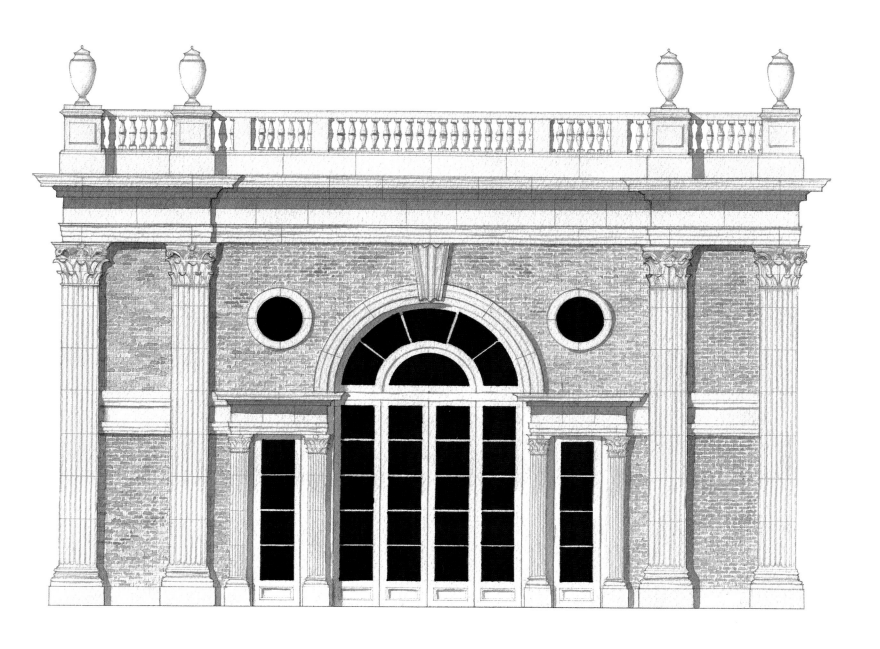

Watercolor study of a wing facade

159

1

2

3

Fig. 1: Ogden Mills House, Staatsburg, New York, 1897, McKim, Mead & White
Fig. 2: Grand Trianon, Versailles, France, 1708, Jules Hardouin-Mansart and Louis Le Vau
Fig. 3: Frederick William Vanderbilt House, Hyde Park, New York, 1899, McKim, Mead & White

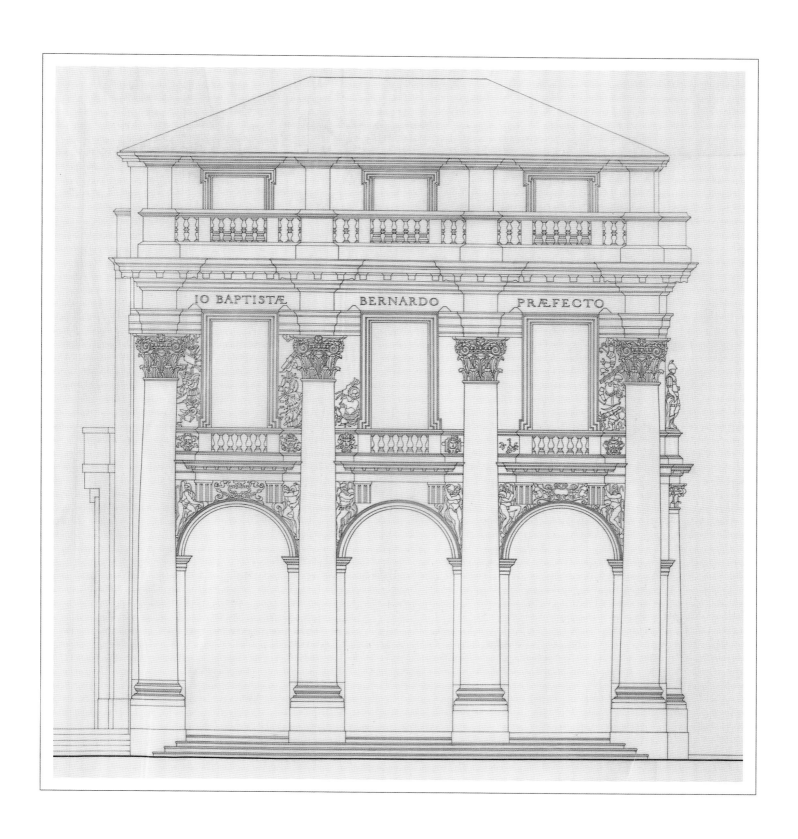

Elevation of the Loggia del Capitaniato, Vicenza, Italy, 1572, Andrea Palladio

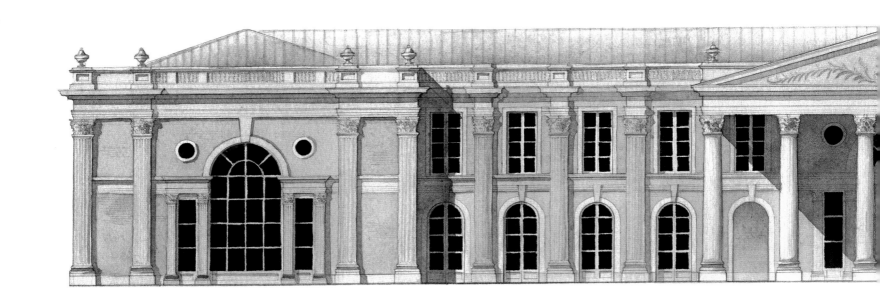

Watercolor study of the front facade

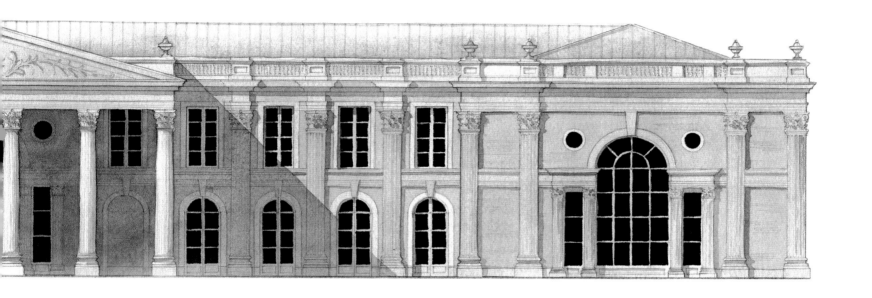

GEORGIAN ARCHITECTURE

Georgian architecture is found the world over. In its purest form, it is found in Great Britain. Regional versions are found in British colonies, a great example of which is the Lutyens' Delhi neighborhood in New Delhi, India. The Renaissance in England saw the influence of Palladio first popularized by Inigo Jones. Chiswick House, Chatsworth, and Blenheim Palace are all fine examples of symmetrical building plans for seemingly untamed and natural sites. This is a distinctly English way of building, and is also reflected in the picturesque gardens that were laid out to idealize the organic natural landscape.

In America, vernacular seventeenth- and eighteenth-century versions of Georgian architecture are found in Williamsburg, Virginia, and other colonial towns. Though usually made up of a simple box of brick or wood cladding, the designs are often symmetrical, with decorative crown moldings, cornices, and entry doors framed by columns topped with a pediment.

The nineteenth century brought the Classical and Greek Revivals. Double-height columns were often used to order the facades, referencing the massive columnar designs of antiquity. Detailing became heavily influenced by the archaeological discoveries of the time, with Greek precedents supplanting Roman detailing over time.

A CLASSICAL REVIVAL TOWNHOUSE

O NE OF WESTERN AESTHETICS'S MAJOR ASSETS IS
the manipulation of proportions. It can be dangerous, as the smallest change can result in a disastrous
proportional relationship, making it a fine line to walk. One works either within the rules in an unruly
way, or the opposite. This is why I particularly enjoyed designing this townhouse. Compared to its
neighbors, it's small and narrow, sitting modestly back from the street. Yet with four double-height
Doric columns sitting upon a plinth facing the street, it resembles a small temple to a Greek goddess.

I had the good fortune to obtain this unique commission from a young bachelor. Though single at
the time, he made sure that his program included ample closet space for his future wife and bedrooms
for their children. His foresight paid off, as his wife just gave birth to their first child.

The site is located on a block where many Classical houses face a park to the south and have great
views of a bay to the north. A modern home with a large cantilever supported by a pier sits to the east,
while a Georgian apartment building sits to the west. One of the goals for the design was to bridge this
gap, creating a dialogue between the two neighboring buildings. Another factor was that the client,
a passionate car and motorcycle collector, desired a large garage for storage and repairs. In order to
reconcile these various design factors without encroaching on the rear garden (another requirement),
a unique solution was required.

As a student at Cooper Union, I had frequently walked by the mid-1830s LaGrange Terrace on
Lafayette Street in New York [*p. 168, Fig. 2*]. Inspired by this monumental portico set a story above the
ground, I pulled the garage forward to the front of the house to create a double-height portico above
it. Because the garage creates a plinth for the Doric porch, this move allowed for a larger garage that
contributes to the design rather than detracts from it, and reflects the three-dimensional character of
the modern facade to the east [*p. 167*].

The two-story pergola of Doric columns raised above the street level creates a powerful facade
which far exceeds the size of the relatively small site, similar to the Roper House (1838) in Charleston,

Opposite: Front elevation

166

South Carolina [*p. 168, Fig. 1*]. Traditionally, this type of townhouse would have a solid roof overhanging the outdoor terrace but climactic conditions dictated an open trellis. Based on the Denticular Doric order of Vignola, an entablature was pulled apart to create the various portions of the supporting beam and rafters that make up the trellis [*p. 170*]. An architrave with a truncated frieze and partial cornice forms the supporting beam, taking the place of a traditional architrave. The rafters sit on top of this beam, creating a placeholder for the nonexistent frieze. Finally, a larger scale cornice lies above this, flush with the building itself, to complete the abstracted entablature.

At the ground floor, a broken, arched pediment above the entry door is juxtaposed against a simple, segmental arched door which was inspired by the George F. Baker House [*p. 170; p. 172, Figs. 4 and 6; p. 173*]. This reflects the elaborate entry sequence through the galleries to the stair hall as opposed to the simple, utilitarian garage articulated with carriage house doors [*p. 169; p. 174, Fig. 8*]. Moving up to the first floor, the doors reflect a true piano nobile, or the most important floor in a classical design. Alternating triangular and arched pedimented doors puncture the facade, representing the family room found within and the living room beyond. Less emphasis is given to the upper windows, as befits the more private, secondary bedrooms found within.

Located in the center of the residence, with interior design by Martha Angus, the stair hall serves as a monumental entry for a site that would not accommodate a large entry hall. The space itself is three stories tall. A circular skylight supports lanterns hanging from a central chain which serve to draw the viewer's eye up to the laylight above [*p. 174, Figs. 7 and 9; p. 175*]. This stair hall serves as the central organizing feature from which all the major spaces are accessed.

Fig. 1: Roper House, 9 East Battery, Charleston, 1838, Charles Friedrich Reichardt
Fig. 2: LaGrange Terrace, Lafayette Street, New York, early 1830s, Alexander Jackson Davis, Ithiel Town, and James Darkin

1   *2*

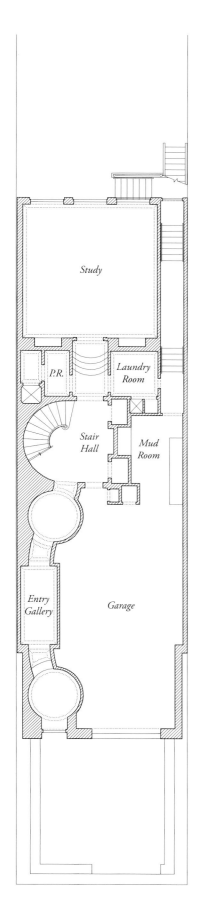

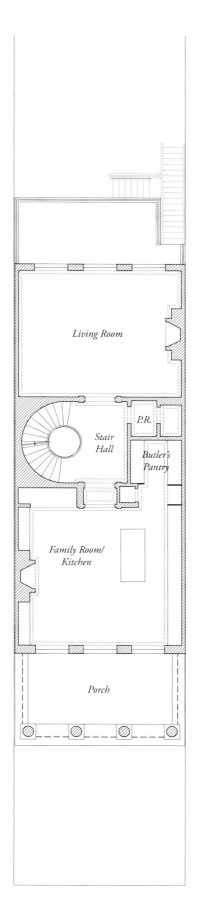

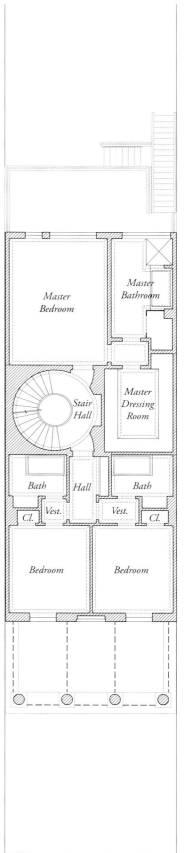

Ground floor plan

First floor plan

Second floor plan

0'   5'   10'

Above: Watercolor study of the front facade *Opposite:* View of the park from the Doric porch

3

4

5

6

Fig. 3: Denticular Doric order, sixteenth century, Vignola *Fig. 4:* Watercolor study of the front entry door
Fig. 5: Carriage house door at the George F. Baker House, 67 East 93rd Street, 1932, Delano and Aldrich
Fig. 6: Entry door at the George F. Baker House, 67 East 93rd Street, 1932, Delano and Aldrich ***Opposite:*** Entry door

7

8

9

Fig. 7: View of the stair hall and lay light above
Fig. 8: Gallery
Fig. 9: Stair hall at the ground floor
Opposite: A view of the stair hall from the second floor. The steel palings, painted satin black, are topped with a curved mahogany handrail. The lanterns are hung in series, which was inspired by the Palace of the Abbot (1789) at the Abbey of Royaumont, near Paris. That building was designed by Louis Le Masson, a student of Claude-Nicolas Ledoux, for the Abbé Le Cornut de Balivière, a chaplain to Louis XVI.

A COLONIAL COUNTRY HOUSE

WHAT MOVES ME ABOUT THIS HOUSE IS ITS purely American style. The white wooden house with green shutters suggests the houses of the Founding Fathers. Grand, but simple, their houses reflected their personal philosophies. Their homes, I believe, are among the greatest treasures of this country. The family that commissioned this house was fascinated by these colonial treasures, and wanted a large house that would retain the feel of a smaller scale, eighteenth-century Georgian house. To achieve this, the massing of the house is broken into three parts: the main house, the hyphen, and dependency or carriage house.

Looking at the front facade, the original portion appears to be an elegant two-story house with a pedimented entry, similar to the one at the eighteenth-century Belle Isle Plantation in South Carolina [*p. 177; p. 181, Fig. 3*]. Supported by two pairs of Doric columns, a broken entablature supports a pediment with an arched ceiling [*pp. 182–83*]. Three dormers and two pairs of chimneys create a sense of verticality, offsetting the otherwise rigid horizontal layout of the windows. One of these chimneys is not functional, but it was necessary to maintain symmetry. This facade represents the public spaces of the house on the ground level and the family's bedrooms above. The rear facade is also symmetrical, with a smaller pedimented door and window above similar to the Windsor House (1801) by Asher Benjamin in Windsor, Vermont [*p. 181, Fig. 2; pp. 184–85*]. This window is one of my favorite details, and was placed so that it was centered on the stair hall landing [*p. 189*]. Its location creates a focal point that pulls the viewer through the interior space up to the first floor, and also modulates the exterior facade in a lively way [*p. 180; p. 186, Fig. 7; p. 188, Fig. 8*].

The hyphen adjacent to the main block of the house reads as an addition to the main residence. It contains a large kitchen and pantries on the ground floor and a children's family room on the first floor. A simple gabled roof extends from the main house with dormers allowing light into the children's family room. The mud room allows the children easy access to and from the gardens, as

Opposite: View of the entrance hall

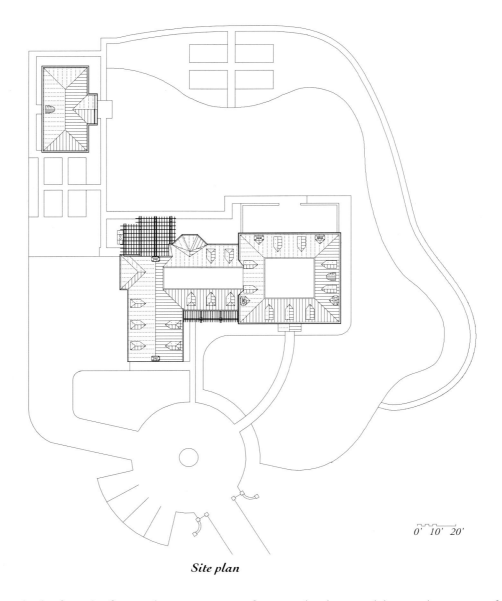

Site plan

well as access for the whole family from the garage. Befitting the less public and more informal part of the family residence, this portion of the house is shielded from the front by a screen of Doric columns supporting a pergola.

The carriage house wing connects to the hyphen and is designed to look more rustic than the rest of the house. This is reflected in its more informal plan which houses the garage on the ground floor and the guest bedroom above. Large segmental arched carriage-house doors with glass panes puncture the side of the building, creating a charming side entry to the garage and keeping it out of the view from the street [*p. 186, Fig. 5, 6*]. At the front of the building, the window spacing is based on the slope of the roof. Along with two nonfunctioning chimneys, this creates a simple facade for this wing of the house. A pergola and outdoor fireplace are located at the rear. These additions, along with the protruding octagonal form of the breakfast room, break up the mass of the rear elevation and balance the asymmetrical composition.

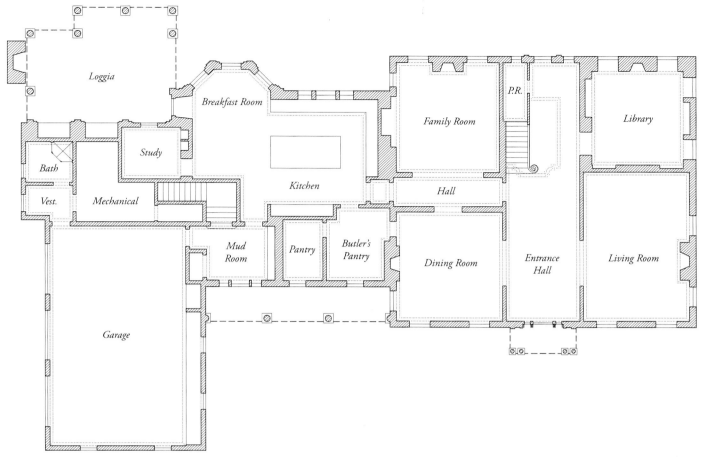

Loggia

Breakfast Room

Study

Bath

Vest.

Mechanical

Kitchen

Family Room

P.R.

Library

Hall

Mud Room

Pantry

Butler's Pantry

Dining Room

Entrance Hall

Living Room

Garage

Ground floor plan

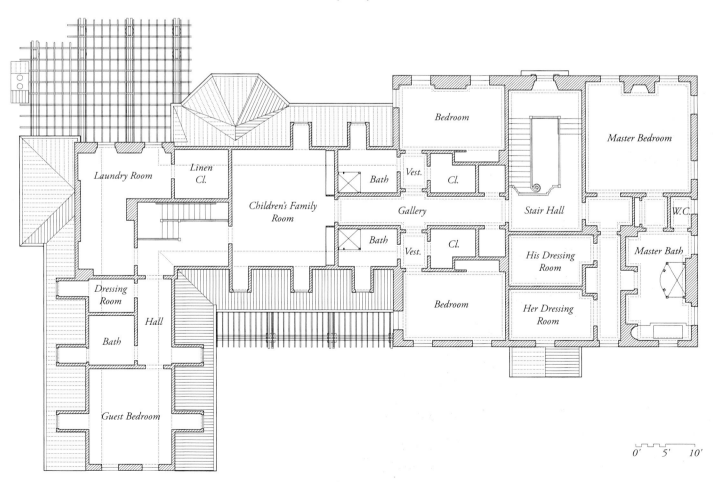

Bedroom

Master Bedroom

Laundry Room

Linen Cl.

Bath

Vest.

Cl.

Stair Hall

W.C.

Children's Family Room

Gallery

His Dressing Room

Master Bath

Bath

Vest.

Cl.

Dressing Room

Bedroom

Her Dressing Room

Hall

Bath

Guest Bedroom

0'   5'   10'

First floor plan

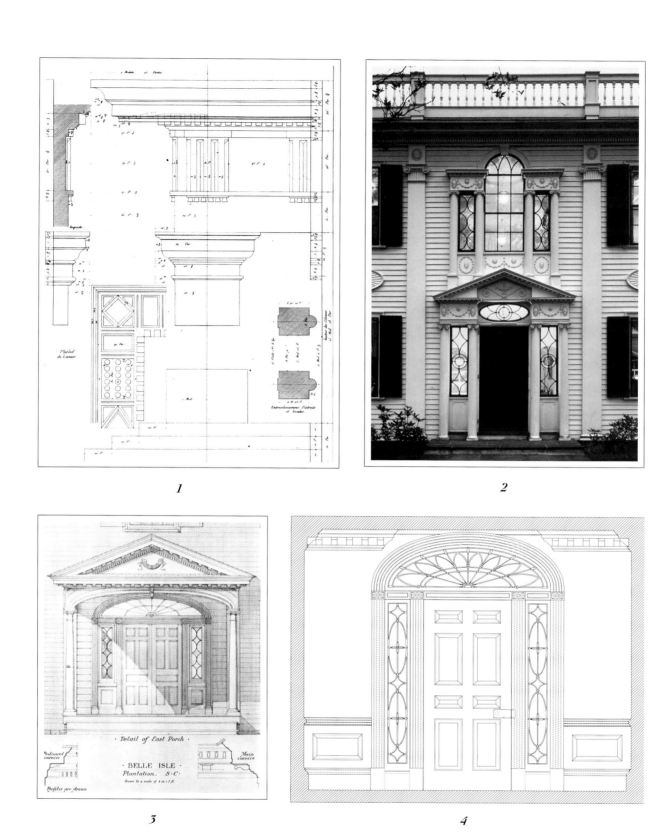

Fig. 1. Doric order from the Theater of Marcellus in Rome **Fig. 2.** Entry facade of the Windsor House, Windsor, Vermont, 1801, Asher Benjamin. Photograph by Paul Rocheleau, image courtesy *The Magazine ANTIQUES*
Fig. 3. Detail of the east porch of Belle Isle, near Georgetown, South Carolina, mid-1930s **Fig. 4.** Entry door detail

Watercolor study of the front facade

Watercolor study of the garden facade

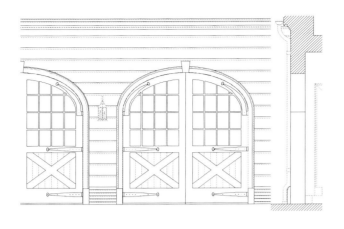

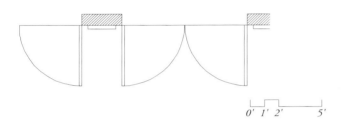

5

6

7

Fig. 5: Carriage house door detail
Fig. 6: View of the side elevation of the carriage house
Fig. 7: Detail of the rear elevation
Opposite: View of the rear elevation

0' 1' 2'   5'

Fig. 8: Arched window at the stair hall landing *Fig. 9:* Lay light above the stair hall
Fig. 10: Detail of the stair stringer *Fig. 11:* Detail drawing of the stair stringer
Opposite: Interior elevation of the stair hall

0'   1'   2'   5'

189

Above: Mudroom *Opposite*: View of the family room

AN AMERICAN COUNTRY HOUSE

S QUARE, CLEAN AND SIMPLE, THIS IS THE CLASSIC
American Colonial style house updated with every modern amenity. While the house uses classical language, it is not overly ornamental. Per the client's request, it was kept fairly simple. It is an indoor-outdoor house for a growing family, with plenty of exterior gathering spaces close to nature.

To retain a certain level of sophistication, the Doric order was used throughout the house to bring depth to the design while, at the same time, keeping it relatively simple [p. 194, Fig. 2; p. 198, Fig. 6]. Bright white siding and plaster detailing, along with the Eastern white cedar shingle roof, adds contrast to the crisp design [p. 196–97]. The use of greenery on the exterior, with pairs of large basins containing neat plants and flowers flanking the entrances, gives the doors a sense of importance without requiring ostentatious ornamentation [p. 194, Fig. 1].

The clients have three children, and as such wanted the rear garden and pool to be major focal points in the design. The dining, living, family, and breakfast rooms all look out on the rear garden and have ample access to the exterior [p. 200–01]. A trellised portico creates an outdoor space for the living room centered on the pool, while another nearby trellis creates an attractive spot to lay out, completing the view from the living room.

Special attention was given to the circular pavilion designed as a sheltered outdoor living and dining area adjoining the breakfast room [p. 193]. The design for this pavilion is based on that of the Pavillon des Fleurs (1687) in Marly, France, by the atelier Jules Hardouin-Mansart [p. 198, Fig. 5]. Instead of using columns to support the entablature and roof, the design employs curved pillars based on the Doric order [p. 198, Fig. 7]. These create a solid structure that supports the large bell-shaped dome [p. 199]. The exterior roof is made of cedar shingles, while the interior has a painted polygonal bell-shaped beadboard ceiling.

Opposite: Outdoor dining pavilion

1

2

3

4

Figs. 1 and 2: Side entry at the mud room *Fig. 3:* Window detail *Fig. 4:* Detail of an exterior door
Opposite: View of the pool trellis and rear garden from the outdoor pavilion
Following pages: View of the rear garden elevation

5

6

7

Fig. 5: Pavillon des Fleurs,
Marly, France, 1687, atelier Jules
Hardouin-Mansart. Watercolor by
Andrew Zega and Bernd H. Dams
Fig. 6: Detail of the intersection
between a Doric column and pilaster
Fig. 7: Detail of a curved pillar at
the outdoor pavilion
Opposite: Watercolor study of the
outdoor pavilion
Following pages: Living room

A DUPLEX PENTHOUSE APARTMENT

LIGHT IS THIS PENTHOUSE APARTMENT'S greatest treasure. It flows in from large projecting window bays, picture windows, a porthole window, and laylights, and is reflected by matte white paneling and waxed, aged parquet de Versailles. Inspired by Robert Adam, the architecture is highly articulated. White fluted pilasters, rosettes, high ceilings, and arches in enfilade make a definitively classical statement, yet convey a modern feeling of openness. When modern sensibility meets the complexity of eighteenth-century English forms, this is what happens.

Before beginning the design, the apartment was gutted. Upon entering the apartment through the elevator lobby and entrance vestibule, one passes into the entrance hall. A translucent round porthole window, inspired by the eighteenth-century Hôtel d'Orrouer in Paris by Pierre Boscry, is located at the stair to bring natural light from the alley located between this building and the next [p. 205, Figs. 1 and 2]. Doric pilasters, inspired by the fourth-century Baths of Diocletian in Rome, regularize the space while a gracefully curved stair with a solid banister creates a complex form and adds tension to the otherwise rectilinear space [p. 203; p. 205, Fig. 3; p. 207]. A blind door, hidden within the paneling, opens to a guest bedroom.

Through this entrance hall is a long gallery which has a new laylight above, made possible by its location on the top floor [p. 206]. A series of arches punctuate the long horizontal space as you walk through to the living room and dining room. In the living room, furniture by the interior designers Andrew Fisher and Jeffry Weisman complements the design. Great attention was paid to details; the room features a commode with moldings that match the wainscoting of the architecture [p. 207, Fig. 6].

Opposite: View of the entrance vestibule

A projecting bay with picture windows is articulated as a separate space adjacent to the living room [*p. 209*]. A pair of arched niches adjacent to the fireplace create a focal point for the room.

Following the client's desire for a clean, classical design, the floor plan is very open. Large arches allow easy movement between living and dining rooms and a modern expression of space, while retaining the classical demarcation of distinct spaces for different functions [*p. 208*]. Inspired by the dining room at the Saltram House (1768) by Robert Adam, an octagonal dining room was created with four niches on the corners that feels intimate yet is open to both the breakfast room and living room [*p. 207, Figs. 5, 7*]. The kitchen is accessed by another of these arches, which can be closed off by a pair of mirrored French sliding doors. This opens a view from the kitchen, through the dining room, to the water, and lets the host close the kitchen when entertaining formally.

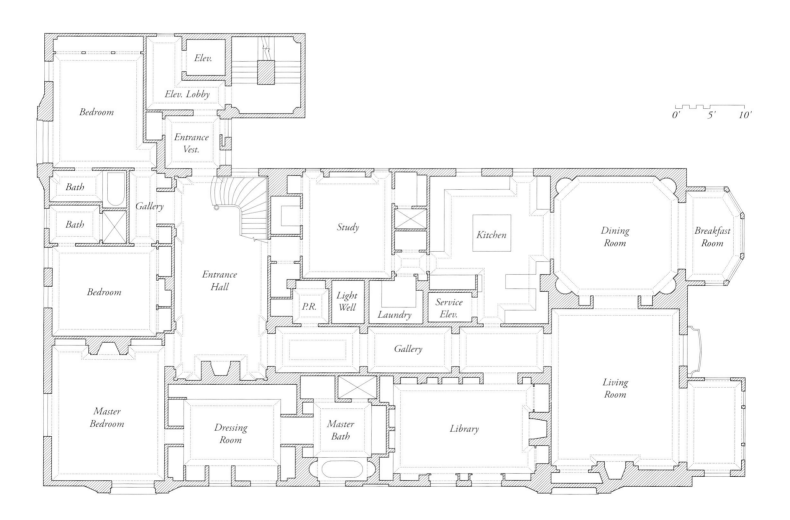

Above: Apartment floor plan *Fig. 1:* View of a portal window in the entrance hall *Fig. 2:* Main staircase of the Hotel d'Orrouer, Paris, France, early eighteenth century, Pierre Boscry *Fig. 3:* Entrance hall

1

2

3

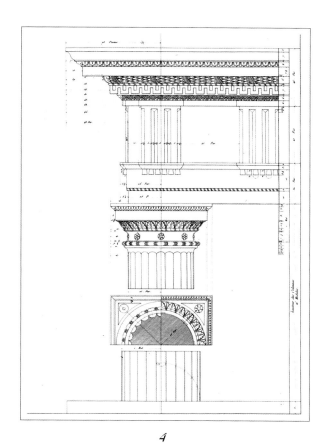

4

5

6

7

Fig. 4: Doric order from the Baths of Diocletian, Rome, Italy, 306 CE
Fig. 5: Dining room of the Saltram House, Devon, England, 1768, Robert Adam *Fig. 6:* Detail of the living room
Fig. 7: View of the dining room beyond *Opposite:* Gallery with the lay light above

Above: Arched entry to the living room *Opposite:* Living room

A GEORGIAN COTTAGE

T HE COUPLE WHO BUILT THIS HOUSE LIVED MOST of their adult lives in this area, raised a family here, and now their children are following suit. Having already built a family retreat a few hours out into the country, they wanted a small but elegant house, close to town, in order to spend more time with their children and grandchildren. They chose a site within walking distance of the town center, and the design reflects this decision.

Befitting a couple with grown children, the program for the house was minimal. The entrance hall is located at the front of the house and leads into the great room, on axis with a fireplace that serves as a focal point [*p. 213*]. The great hall, with interior design by Suzanne Tucker, is a large, inviting space that the couple uses for entertaining. Adjacent to this space is a large kitchen with an informal dining area [*p. 212*]. Both theses spaces, along with the master suite, are over-scaled for the size of the house due to the clients' lifestyle.

Olive green and gray siding, cedar shingle roofs, green shutters, and crisp Classical detailing were used to create the elevations [*pp. 214–15*]. This is what true American design is about: simplicity and

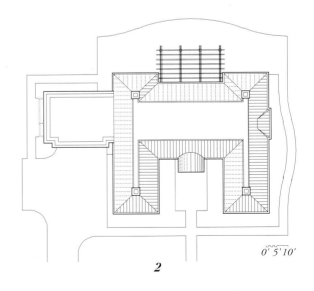

1

2

0' 5' 10'

Fig. 1: Residence for W. C. Holman Jr., Albany, Georgia, 1948, Edward Vason Jones *Fig. 2:* Site plan
Opposite, above: Front entrance facade and gardens ***Opposite, below:*** Detailed view of the curved, pedimented entrance portico

Watercolor study of the front facade

A CITY RESIDENCE

A CLASSIC AMERICAN HOUSE BUILT BETWEEN 1898 and 1911 stood on this site until is destruction in the late 1940s. A house was constructed in its place in 1951, designed in the so-called "Contemporary style" of the time. Needless to say, this style did not age gracefully, and stuck out like a sore thumb in a neighborhood otherwise composed entirely of original houses built at the time of the initial development. The client had the house razed. I had the good fortune to have designed an addition to one of the other houses in the neighborhood that had caught their eye, and they asked me build a house for them that would fit in perfectly with the turn-of-the-century houses in the neighborhood.

As a big fan of William Lawrence Bottomley (1883–1951), my design for this residence was inspired by one of his houses in Richmond, Virginia, from 1916 [*p. 218*]. The elevation is composed of four bays, with the entrance door located at the far right [*p. 219*]. This is how the Bottomley house is ordered, though the detailing here is very different. This entrance door sits under an arch supported by Doric pilasters and is further framed by two pairs of larger pilasters engaged into one another to denote the main entry [*p. 217*]. Each of the French doors on the front elevation has a full entablature capping it, revealing the importance of the ground level. After entering into the front hall, one passes into the impressive double-height entrance hall. This references the same Bottomley house as precedent [*p. 220*]. The hall orders the ground floor and allows movement through the dining room, living room, or family room, with interior design by Ken Fulk Design [*pp. 224–25*].

At the rear elevation of this level sits a columnar screen with glass infill [*p. 227*]. This allows the dining terrace, family room, and breakfast room to have open views to the garden while retaining the classical nature of the design [*p. 222, Fig. 4*]. The columnar level of the elevation is supported on a

Opposite: Arched entrance door with surrounding pilasters supporting a full entablature

heavily rusticated basement floor. The rustication and simple punched openings reflect the change in elevation and the utilitarian spaces on this level. The playroom is located here in order to allow the children easy access to the garden.

The first floor contains the master bedroom and study at the front, with the children's bedrooms at the rear [*p. 225*]. A string course creates a distinction in the elevation between the public and private portions of the house. Sitting on top of this string course, the casement windows line up with the French doors below. At the rear garden elevation, the windows are organized into three groups. The two larger groupings to the outside are placed for views from the bedrooms, while the smaller central window allows for a view out from the gallery on that level.

The second floor is composed of utility spaces and the guest bedroom. Three dormers are centered on the solid areas of the first floor's elevation to allow light and air into the attic space. They also add movement and verticality to an otherwise strictly horizontal facade. At the rear elevation, a negative dormer was created for the guest-bedroom terrace. Two chimneys, one functional as the living room fireplace and the other for aesthetic balance, are located at either side of the elevation [*p. 226*].

Front elevation of 2309 Monument Avenue, Richmond, Virginia, 1916, William Lawrence Bottomley
Opposite: Front elevation

218

1

2

3

Fig. 1: Skylight and chandelier
in the entrance hall
Fig. 2: Entrance hall stair
Fig. 3: Stair hall of 2309
Monument Avenue, Richmond,
Virginia, 1916, William
Lawrence Bottomley
Opposite: Back stair from above

4

Fig. 4: View of the dining
terrace
Fig. 5: The master bath
Following pages: View of the
entrance hall with the front
hall and living room beyond

5

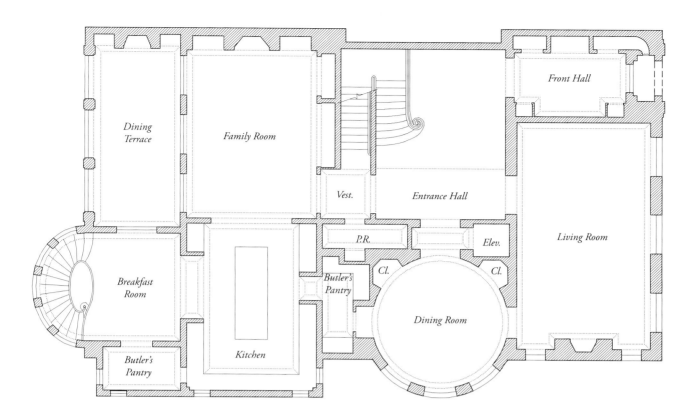

Ground floor plan

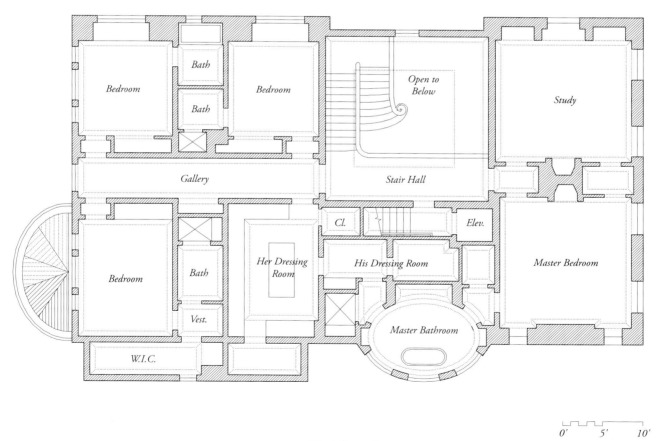

First floor plan

Above: Watercolor study of the front facade *Opposite:* The rear garden elevation

AN ANGLO-GRECIAN COUNTRY HOUSE

T HE SITE WAS ONE THOUSAND ACRES OF undeveloped land, free of any trace of humanity. We drove there on rough dirt roads until suddenly, cresting a hill, the perfect location for this house was revealed within a grove of old oaks. Think of Andrew Wyeth's *Christina's World*, a rolling brown and yellow landscape, and add beautiful oak trees [*p. 228, Fig. 1*].

In 1847, William H. Ranlett published a pattern book for an Anglo-Grecian Villa in *Godey's Lady's Book* [*p. 228, Fig. 2*]. The house shown in this design has an extended octagonally shaped hall in the center of the butterfly shaped plan. The parlor, dining room, drawing room, and library are located in each of the four wings of the ground floor. These wings extend out to create a modified Greek cross plan

1

2

Fig. 1: *Christina's World*, 1948, Andrew Wyeth
Fig. 2: Perspective of the Anglo-Grecian Villa or Cooleemee Plantation House, between Mocksville and Lexington, North Carolina, 1847, William H. Ranlett **Opposite:** The house at dusk

with porches between them. Four bedrooms are located above each of the rooms that make up the four wings. While this exact design was never built, a similar house, also based upon Ranlett's publication, was built at Cooleemee between Mocksville and Lexington in North Carolina.

The name Cooleemee comes from the Native American tribe that lived there, which in their native tongue meant "the place where the white oaks grow." Coincidentally, the site chosen for this house is also a place where oaks grow. After visiting Cooleemee and falling in love with the design, the clients wanted a house with a very similar feel. In fact, this butterfly-shaped plan, with its four symmetrical sides, works perfectly at the top of a bluff [*p. 229*].

Though the clients wanted a house that evoked the feeling of Cooleemee, they did not want a replica. Instead, the published design that the North Carolina house was based on was studied, revised, and updated for them. Cooleemee utilized an elongated octagonal shape for the central stair hall. In our design, the elongated octagon was regularized into a true octagon [*p. 234*]. The stair hall was then topped with an octagonal dome inspired by Thomas Jefferson's Monticello (1772) in Charlottesville, Virginia [*pp. 235, 236, 237*]. From this central room one can access the kitchen, dining room, library, and living room. The forms of these rooms were again regularized into squares. The master bedroom and bath take up two of the wings on the first floor, while a study and guest bedroom make up the other two. The detailing fabricated by Bret Hull throughout the house was inspired by the published drawings with refinements and modifications made to idealize those forms.

An unusual project, the owner decorated it in pastel colors [*p. 238, Figs. 3 and 4*]. Blue and white on the outside, blue and pink on the interior, the house feels distinctly nineteenth century. The English character of the architecture is contrasted with these distinctly French colors, those of Marie Antoinette or the painter Marie Laurencin. This nineteenth-century character might be tomorrow's new trend, as this was a period of treasures that many might look back on fondly in the future.

Opposite: Detailed view of the front porch

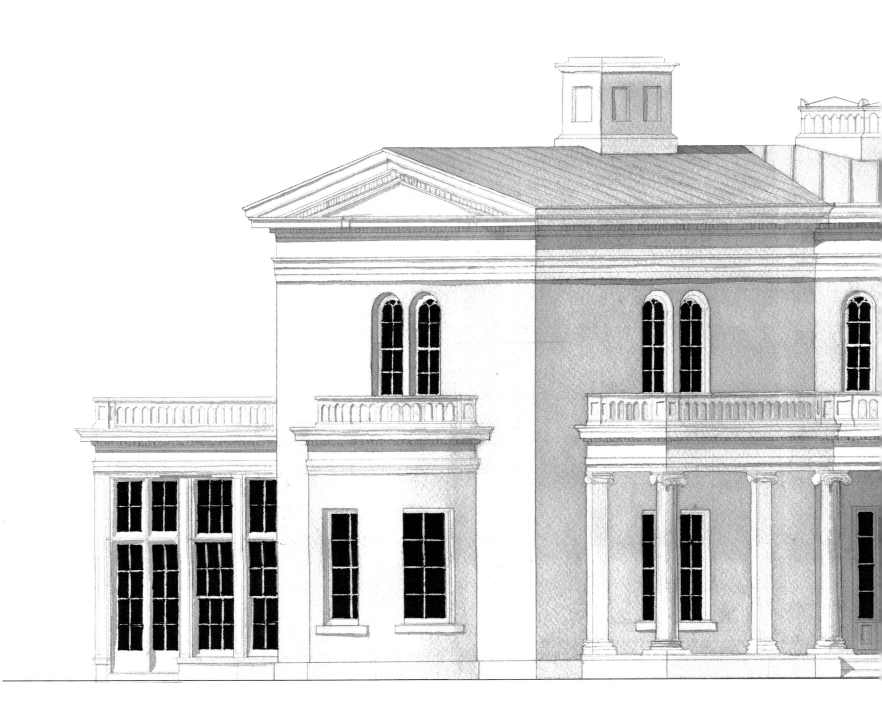

Watercolor study of the front facade

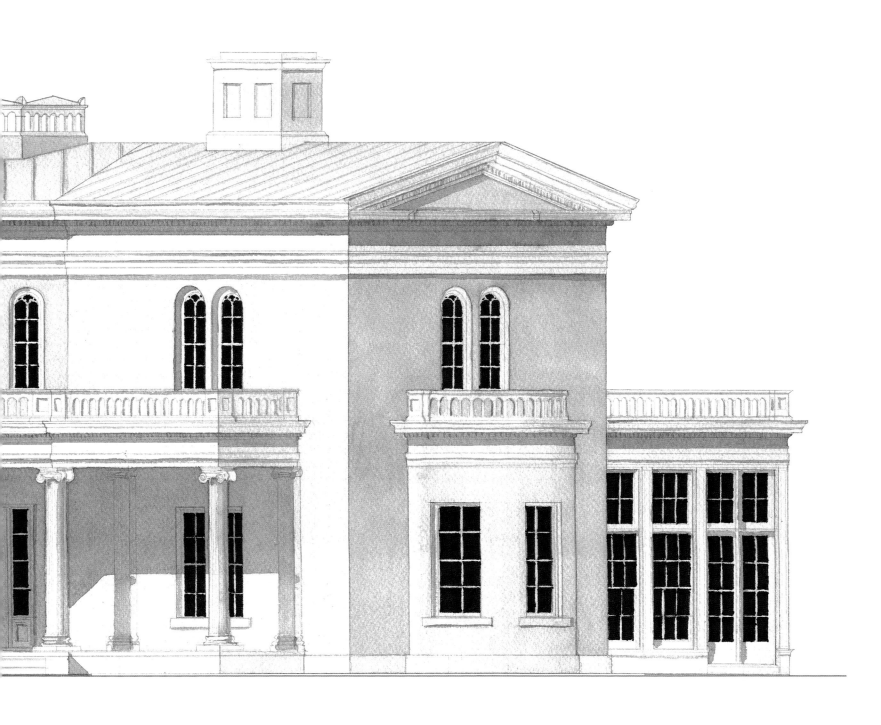

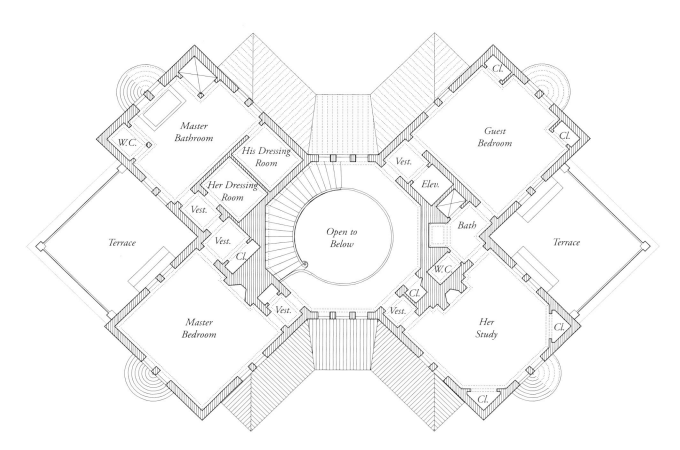

First floor plan

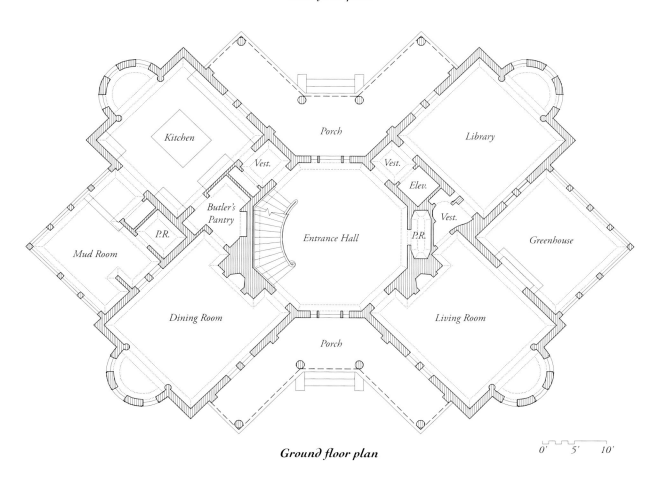

Ground floor plan

0'   5'   10'

234

Watercolor study of the entrance hall

Above: View of the entrance hall *Opposite:* Octagonal dome and oculus

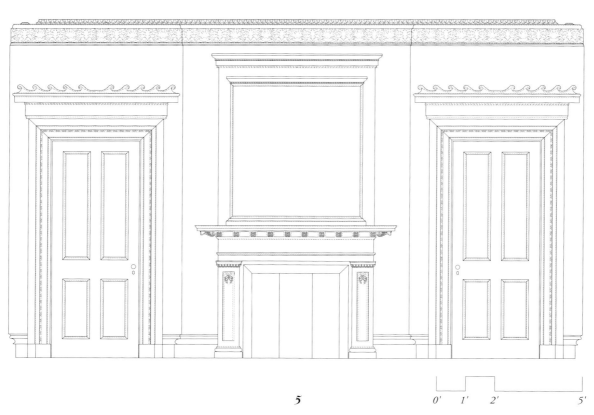

3   4

5

0'   1'   2'   5'

Fig. 3: Powder room door *Fig. 4:* Detail of the library *Fig. 5:* Living room interior elevation
Opposite: Living room fireplace *Following pages:* View of the house and oak groves

GLOSSARY OF TERMS

ACROTERION: an ornament placed at one of the three points of a pediment

AMPHITHEATER: an oval- or circular-shaped space with stepped seating, often used for public entertainment, originating in ancient Rome and based upon the Greek theater

ARCHITRAVE: the lowest portion of the entablature in a classical order corresponding to the major beam in a structural composition

ARTICULATED: differentiated; the separation of different elements

ASYMMETRICAL: when the elements of one half of a structure do not replicate the forms of the other half

BASE: the lowest portion of a classical column; or, the lowest portion of a building that sits directly on the ground, often made of stone

BATTERED: describing walls that slope outward to add strength and solidarity to the building's composition

BAY: a typical portion of a regularized facade, as in a vertical grouping of windows with columns on either side that is repeated throughout a facade design

BEADBOARD: wood siding laid out in a vertical manner

BLIND DOOR: a hidden door, designed to meld into the wall, with its moldings flush with those of the wainscoting, paneling, and crown moldings

BOOKEND: to place a mass at the side of a composition to terminate and hold an edge

BUTTERFLY PLAN: a floor layout that is shaped of a central portion from which four rooms or wings extend in the shape of a butterfly's wings

CABOCHON: a diamond-or circular-shaped piece of a floor pattern defining the floor's grid

CASEMENT WINDOW: a window attached to its frame by hinges on one side

CHARACTER: the essence of a building placing it within the context of its setting; often made most obvious through detailing, massing, and its construction materials

CHEVRON PATTERN: a floor pattern laid out in a series of angled pieces to make a V pattern

CIRCULATION: the paths of movement through rooms and spaces

CLADDING: the exterior material of the building that is not an integral structural component, such as stone veneer, wood siding, etc.

CLASSICAL:

    ARCHITECTURE: that which is rooted in the tradition of ancient Greece and Rome, sometimes with Egyptian and other near-Eastern influences. Architecture drawing inspiration from the past, along with its location and context, to define its modern design. Often utilizes one of the five orders in its proportioning system or design.

    LANGUAGE: the common elements and proportions used to create a classical design; there is a correct and incorrect way to use these elements, and certain forms are used to define the use of the interior space. This allows a classically trained architect to understand the use and purpose of the building through its design and iconography.

    ORDER: one of the five columnar orders, made up of a columnar type with its respective base, capital, entablature, detailing, and proportioning system. See *Column* for the five orders.

COFFER: an indented portion of a ceiling, often with moldings surrounding it; creates interest in the ceiling and a hierarchy of beams and rafters due to its spacing

COLISEUM: the amphitheater in Rome built by the Flavian emperors from 72–80 CE; in modern times it describes a large amphitheater or other stepped space with a large central portion used for entertainment

COLONNADE: two rows of columns, often covered, that form a promenade

COLOSSAL: massive in scale; in architectural terms, this often refers to either double- or triple-height columns (as in those that rise two or three floor heights) or a proportioning system that is beyond the human scale

COLUMN: a vertical structural element often supporting an entablature that has a base, shaft, and capital

    TUSCAN: a Roman columnar order thought to be derived from Etruscan temples; a simplified version of the Doric order

DORIC: a Greek columnar order with a simple capital, alternating triglyphs and metopes in the frieze, and without a base. This order corresponds to the male figure.

IONIC: a Greek columnar order with a capital made up of two scrolls. In its pure form it is directional, with a front and back with two sides. This order corresponds to the mature female figure.

CORINTHIAN: a Greek columnar order with a capital made up of stylized acanthus leaves and a shaft that is often fluted. This order corresponds to the young, slender figure of a maiden.

COMPOSITE: a derivative of the Corinthian columnar order seen during the late Roman Empire, and separated from the Corinthian by Renaissance architects. The capital is made up of stylized acanthus leaves with scrolls at the top portion of the capital. This order corresponds to the young, slender figure of the maiden, and was often used for churches of the Virgin Mary during the Renaissance.

ENGAGED: a column that is not a complete circle in plan, and is connected to a wall or other vertical structural element

COMMODE: a piece of furniture, often a low cabinet with drawers or doors for storage

CONSOLE: a corbel; a structural or decorative element jutting out from the surface of the wall to support a projecting horizontal member

CORNICE: the uppermost portion of a classical entablature

DEMARCATION: distinction between various elements

DEPENDENCY: a secondary or tertiary building housing subordinate functions to those of the main residence or building

DIALOGUE: the interaction that buildings have with one another in terms of style, the borrowing of elements and proportions, and location within the continuity of history

DORMER: a window protruding from the main roof, often covered with a small roof

DOVECOTE: a tower or space housing doves or other birds for the purpose of collecting fertilizer

ENFILADE: a series of arches or openings lining up to create an axial view through a series of rooms, used especially in French classical architecture

ENTABLATURE: the horizontal element in a classical order that sits upon columns, made up of an architrave, frieze, and cornice

ESCALIER: French, "stair"

FACADE: a side of a building, often used when talking about the front of a building

FAUX: false, often pertaining to an element of a design that looks real and is used for aesthetic reasons but serves no real function

FINIAL: an element that serves to cap, complete or provide a final accent to a vertical form or element in a design

FOLLY: a small pavilion or temple-like structure built as a place to escape the elements; also used as a focal point or to create a romantic sense of age or decay within an English garden

FOYER: a space near the entrance of a residence or larger space; often used for circulation purposes and less grand than an entrance hall

FRENCH DOOR: a pair of doors that open to either side to allow for a greater unobstructed space at the opening

FRIEZE: the middle portion of the entablature, often decorated or delineated by triglyphs and metopes as in the Doric order

GABLE ROOF: a roof sloped on two sides

GROTTO: a niche, cave or other such space within a natural setting that includes a fountain or other water feature within or around it

HAND SCRAPED: a technique by which flooring is antiqued to give it character and a sense of age

HIERARCHY OF SPACE: the separation of spaces within a design into distinct levels of importance, with the most important being more elaborate and highly articulated than the secondary and tertiary spaces

HINGE: in architectural design, a space or form that serves to mediate between different geometries

HIP ROOF: a roof that slopes down on all sides

HYPHEN: a building that serves as a connecting element between two other buildings, often housing less important and informal spaces

INTEGRAL COLORED PLASTER: stucco that has its color present throughout the mixture; allows the color to remain true as it ages

INTERCOLUMNIATION: the spacing between columns in a classical design

LAY LIGHT: a large glass panel or panels in a ceiling, bringing natural light into a space

LIMESTONE: a sedimentary rock used in building construction and sculptural elements

LOGGIA: a walkway or gallery with columns or piers on one or both sides

MANSARD ROOF: a tall, double pitched roof with a steeper lower portion, made famous by François Mansard in the seventeenth century

MARQUISE: French, "canopy"

METOPE: the rectangular space, ideally a square, between triglyphs in a Doric entablature, often decorated with shields, ox skulls, or some other feature

MODULATE: to vary the proportions in a design or to create different arrangements in a design

MOLDING: a sculptural element extruding along a path to create a distinction between various spaces, planes, or portions of an element

MOTIF: a repetitive element used throughout a composition

NATATIO: a Roman-style swimming pool

NICHE: a recessed portion of a wall, often with a half dome capping it, and found at the termination point of an axis or within a grotto

OCULUS: a circular opening at the center of a dome, as seen at the Pantheon in Rome

ORNAMENT: a non-structural element in composition, without which the design would not convey the same meaning

PANELING: slightly recessed portions of a wall or door adding interest to the composition and punctuating large, flat planes in a composition

PARQUET DE VERSAILLES FLOORING: diagonal squares of decorative wood mosaics, often with patterns that look woven together

PATTERN BOOK: a collection of forms, elements, motifs, and other details used to design buildings within a similar style with ease

PAVILION: a small building, either enclosed (as in the French pavilions of Versailles), or open-aired (as in garden pavilions); in either case these were often used for entertainment or as secondary residences for pleasure

PEDIMENT: a triangular or arched surface sitting upon columns with an entablature running along its top

    BROKEN: a pediment, interrupted partially through the top two sides of the triangle or the arched portion of the form

PERGOLA: a walkway, with columns or pillars on either side supporting beams and rafters for shade

PIANO NOBILE: the most important floor level in a classical design; the first floor above the ground floor

PILASTER: a column that is abstracted into being rectangular in plan and is engaged into a wall

PLASTER: a building material similar to mortar or cement, used as an exterior finish

PLINTH: the square base of a column; a raised surface upon which something sits

PORTE-COCHÈRE: a covered space supported by columns or piers on one side and attached to the building on the opposite; used as a drop-off space protected from the elements for automobiles at the front entrance to a building

PRECEDENT: a building, detail, motif, or other object that serves as inspiration for the design of a building or some portion of it

PROPORTION: the geometric relationship of various elements to one another

PUNCHED OPENING: a simple opening in a wall without any surrounding moldings

QUOIN: the stones at the corner of a building, often rusticated to enhance the impression of a strong corner

RADIAL CHEVRON: a floor pattern, laid so the angled pieces of the chevrons make a star shape, radiating out from the center of the pattern

RAFTER TAIL: a small beam that juts out from the surface of the wall to support the roof overhang

RENAISSANCE: the flowering of the arts in the fourteenth through seventeenth centuries based on the scientific revolution and discoveries of antiquity

ROMAN BATH: a large public building complex, typical of the Roman Republic and Empire, housing various hot and cold pools for bathing and recreation

ROMANESQUE: of or pertaining to the architectural style of Medieval Europe from the sixth through the tenth centuries CE, characterized by semicircular arches

ROSETTE: a small flower or other sculptural detail often seen at the center of a coffer or metope

RUSTICATION: a treatment of stone or wood in such a way that it looks more massive and natural; often used at the corners of buildings for quoins or at the bases of buildings to give it a sense of strength

SCALE: the proportions of a building in relation to the human figure or to other portions of the overall structure, complex or surroundings

SEGMENTAL ARCH: an arch that is not a full half-circle

SERLIAN WINDOW: an arched window with two rectangular side windows attached to it, popularized by Sebastiano Serlio and made famous by Andrea Palladio

SPACE: the volume defined by walls or other architectural elements

    PRIMARY: the most important spaces in a building, the served spaces

    SECONDARY: the second-most important spaces in a building, often serving the primary spaces

    TERTIARY: the third-most important spaces in a building, often serving the secondary spaces

    PUBLIC: the spaces seen by visitors and the general public

    PRIVATE: the spaces seen by the owners, privileged guests, and residents

SPRING POINT: the point where an arch begins, or where a recurring element begins

STRING COURSE: a horizontal band of molding at the exterior of a building that is used to differentiate between various portions of the facade or represent the positioning of the interior floors

STYLE: see *Character*. Often used in place of character, style is better applied to certain motifs and elements that were used during one time in a certain place and are being copied to attain the effect of that particular building or era.

TENSION: in architectural terms, the creation of a dynamic interaction between elements that look as if they want to merge into or disengage from one another

THOLOS: a circular temple or other structure

TIMBERED WALLS: walls made of large pieces of wood

TONNEAU: French, a barrel-shaped room in plan

TRANSOM: the small window above a door

TRIGLYPH: the rectangular-channeled portion of the frieze in a Doric entablature

TRIPARTITE: divided into three distinct parts or portions

TRUNCATED: simplified or stunted, edited

TYPOLOGY: the classification of things into distinct groups based upon their characteristics

URBAN CONTAINMENT: the characteristic of a space being surrounded and defined by various buildings and other elements such as walls, hedges, or columnar screens

UTILITARIAN: having no unnecessary elements, fulfilling only its function

WAINSCOTING: the paneling above the baseboard and below the chair rail

CREDITS

p. 2. Front door at "A French Country House." Photograph by Matthew Millman.

p. 5. Wedding pavilion at "The Resort at Pelican Hill." Courtesy of 2011© Tom Lamb/ Irvine Company.

p. 6. Enfilade entry at "A French Country House." Photograph by Mark Darley.

p. 8. Dining pavilion at "A Hillside Villa." Courtesy of Michal Venera.

p. 10. Cut-Outs: Juan Gris Analysis. 1974–75. Courtesy, The Irwin S. Chanin School of Architecture Archive of The Cooper Union.

p. 12. *The Four Books of Architecture* (Mineola, New York: Dover Publications, Inc., 1965), between 62/63 Plate II.

p. 13. Leather box. Photographs by Paul Hayes.

p. 14. Renovation of a Julia Morgan Apartment, with interior design by Tucker & Marks, Inc. Photograph by Matthew Millman.

p. 16. An art collector's apartment, with interior design by Rebecca Bradley. Photograph by Matthew Millman.

p. 17. A Georgian Library, with interior design by Tucker & Marks, Inc. Photograph by Tim Street-Porter.

p. 18. A new family room for a Julia Morgan apartment, with interior design by Tucker & Marks, Inc. Photograph by Matthew Millman.

p. 21. Renovation of a Julia Morgan apartment, with interior design by Tucker & Marks, Inc. Photograph by Matthew Millman.

p. 23. Entry gallery in a pied-à-terre, with interior design by Fisher Weisman. Photograph by Lisa Romerein.

MEDITERRANEAN ARCHITECTURE

p. 24. Acroterion at "A Greek Villa." Photograph by Mark Darley.

A HILLSIDE VILLA

Project Architect: r. Mark Rushing
Architecture Team: Lisa Marie Milat, Marianne Gruber, Akira Kurihara, Natasha Juliana, Eric Haun, Jeff Eade, Day Hilborn, Viet Truong, Stephen Sutro, Karen Siu, Pierson Jones, Eliot Sutro
Interior Designer: Tucker & Marks, Inc.
General Contractor: Ryan Associates
Landscape Architect: Todd R. Cole Landscape Architect
Photographer: Matthew Millman
Precedent Image Credits:
p. 26. Reproduced by permission from Laurent Kruszyk, *Escaliers Parisiens sous l'Ancien Regíme: L'Apogee de la serrurie* (Paris: Somogy, 2011), 67.
p. 28, Fig. 1. Reproduced by permission from © Roberto Schezen/ Esto, *Palm Beach Houses* (New York: Rizzoli, 1991), 255.
p. 32, Fig. 7. Reproduced by permission from The University Art Museum, UCSB, *George Washington Smith: An Architect's Scrapbook* (Los Angeles: Tailwater Press, 2001), 71.

A GREEK VILLA

Project Architects: David Buergler, Suzette Smith, Akira Kurihara
Architecture Team: Robert Colarusso, Michael Callison, Eric Haun, Timothy Blanchard, Heather Hart
Interior Designer: Tucker & Marks, Inc.
General Contractor: Plath & Company
Landscape Architect: Elizabeth Everdell Garden Design
Photographer: unless noted otherwise, photographs by Mark Darley.
p. 48, 49 and p. 50, Fig. 11. Photographs by Matthew Millman.
Watercolor Rendering: Entry portico and entry portico section by Brendan Hart.
Interior door, rear garden facade and master bedroom by Lauren Hedge.
Precedent Image Credits:
p. 39, Fig. 3. Photograph by Cervin Robinson, reproduced by permission from HABS.
p. 39, Fig. 4, and p. 50, Fig. 10. Reproduced by permission from Martin D. Scott, *La Villa Kérylos* (Paris: Editions de l'Amateur, 1997), 101 and 60.
p. 40, Figs. 5 and 6, and p. 50, Fig. 9. Reproduced by permission from Acanthus Press, *Parallel of the Classical Orders of Architecture* (New York: Acanthus Press, 1998), plates 59, 93, and 12.

AN ITALIANATE LAKESIDE VILLA

Project Architects: Jeff Eade, Eric Haun
Architecture Team: Akira Kurihara, Pierre Guettier, David Hingston, Marianne Badawi, Gloria Day, Birgitte Hovmoller, Michael Bernard
Interior Designer: Brian Murphy
General Contractor: Redhorse Construction
Landscape Architect: SWA Group
Photographer: unless noted otherwise, photographs by David Duncan Livingston.
p. 57. Photograph by Mark Darley.

A SPANISH COLONIAL ESTATE/ UNDER CONSTRUCTION

Project Architect: Pierre Guettier
Architecture Team: Eric Haun, Karen Siu, Stephen Sooter, Akira Kurihara, Bethany Snyder, Steven Wong, Benjamin McGriff
Interior Designer: Tucker & Marks, Inc.
General Contractor: Peninsula Custom Homes
Landscape Architect: Suzman & Cole Design Associates
Photographer: Paul Hayes
Watercolor Rendering: Front facade, rear facade, and guest house facade by Brendan Hart.
Precedent Image Credits:
p. 66. Reproduced by permission from Tim Street-Porter, *Santa Barbara Style* (New York: Rizzoli International Publications, Inc. 2001), 156–57.
p. 72, Figs. 1 and 2. Reprinted from Arthur Byne and Mildred Stapley's *Provincial Houses in Spain* (William Helburn Inc, 1925), plates 74 and 155.
p. 72, Fig. 3. Reproduced by permission from Mike Hayward/ Alamy.
p. 72, Fig. 4. Reproduced by permission from James Chen, *Santa Barbara Style* (New York: Rizzoli International Publications, Inc. 2001), 86–87.
p. 74, Fig. 7. Reproduced by permission from James Chen, *George Washington Smith Architect of the Spanish Colonial Revival* (Utah: Gibbs Smith, Nov. 2005), 123.
p. 74, Fig. 8. Reproduced by permission from © Roberto Schezen/ Esto, *Spanish Splendor: Great Palaces, Castles, and Country Homes* (New York: Rizzoli, 2004), 30.

THE RESORT AT PELICAN HILL

Project Interior Architects: Stephen Sutro, Karen Siu
Interior Architecture Team: Steven Dombrowski, Steve Lieberman, Gloria Day, Sarah Appelman, Heather Hart, Michael Bernard, Michael Metiu, Pierre Guettier, Ed Watkins, David Tu, Jeremy Warms, r. Mark Rushing, Olivier Santoni-Costantini
Architect (unaffiliated exterior): Altevers Associates
Interior Designer: Darrel Schmidt Design Associates
General Contractors: Cuesta Construction, Synder Langston, Wentz Group
Landscape Architect: Burton Landscape Architecture Studio
Photographer: unless noted otherwise, photographs courtesy of Marshall Williams, www.marshallwilliams.com.
p. 77. Courtesy of Craig Fuller.
p. 82, top. Courtesy of Rob Gage Photographer.
p. 88, Fig. 9. Courtesy of 2011 © Tom Lamb/ Irvine Company.
Watercolor Rendering: Outdoor wedding pavilion by Brendan Hart.
Precedent Image Credits:
p. 76. Reproduced by permission from © Roberto Schezen/Esto, *The Palladian Ideal* (New York: Rizzoli, 2000), 113.
p. 80, Fig. 1. Reproduced by permission from Jonathan Wallen, *McKim, Mead & White: The Masterworks* (New York: Rizzoli, November 22, 2003), 228.
p. 80. Fig. 2. © 2011 Marco Delmastro.
p. 84, Fig. 3. Photograph courtesy of Cesare Gerolimetto, *Ville Venete: The Villa Civilization in the Mainland Dominion* (Verona: Arsenale Editrice, 1955), 138–39.
p. 84, Figs. 4 and 5. Reproduced by permission from Acanthus Press, *Parallel of the Classical Orders of Architecture* (New York: Acanthus Press, 1998), plates 25 and 76.
p. 84, Fig. 6. Reproduced by permission from © Roberto Schezen/ Esto, *Italian Splendor: Great Palaces, Castles and Villas* (New York: Rizzoli, 2004), 22.
p. 88. Fig. 10. Photograph by Gerhard Lindemann.

FRENCH ARCHITECTURE

p. 90. Front elevation of a wing at "A Country Residence."
Photograph by Matthew Millman.

A FRENCH COUNTRY HOUSE
Project Architect: Akira Kurihara
Architecture Team: Suzette Smith, Nii Quao,
Timothy Blanchard, David Buergler, Heather
Hart, Natasha Juliana, Eric Haun, Jim
Severson, Karen Siu
Interior Designer: Diane Chapman Interiors
General Contractor: Lencioni Construction
Landscape Architect: Lou Marano
Exterior Furnishings: Munder Skiles
Photographer: Photographs by Mark Darley, p. 105–07.
Photographs by Matthew Millman, p. 93, 98, and 99.
Watercolor Rendering: Front facade by Lauren Hedge.
Rear garden facade by Nicole Bernal-Cisneros.
Precedent Image Credits:
p. 94. Drawing by Paul Hayes.
p. 96, Fig. 1. Reproduced by permission from Paolo Marton, *Andrea Palladio: The Architect in His Time* (New York: Abbeville Press, 2007), 119.
p. 96, Fig. 2. Reproduced by permission from © Wayne Andrews/Esto.
p. 96, Figs. 3 and 4. Reprinted from Leigh French's *The Smaller Houses and Gardens of Versailles from 1680 to 1815* (New Hope, PA: The Pencil Points Press, 1926), 155 and 75.
p. 96, Fig. 5. Reproduced by permission from Jonathan Wallen, *John Russell Pope: Architect of Empire* (New York: Rizzoli, July 15, 1998), 90. Fig. 3–57.
p. 104, Fig. 14. Reproduced by permission from imagebroker/Alamy
p. 104, Fig. 15. Reproduced by permission from Roger-Viollet/The Image Works, Inc., *Paris XIXE Siecle l'Immeuble et la Rue,* (Vanves: Hazan, 1997), 247.
p. 104, Fig. 16. Reproduced by permission from JOHN KELLERMAN/Alamy.
p. 104, Figs. 17 and 18. Reproduced by permission from Laurent Kruszyk, *Escaliers Parisiens sous l'Ancien Regime: L'Apogee de la serrurie* (Paris: Somogy, 2011), 76 and 120.

A CITY APARTMENT
Project Architect: Stephen Sutro
Architecture Team: Akira Kurihara, William
Wilson, Day Hilborn
Interior Designer: Tucker & Marks, Inc.
General Contractor: Forde-Mazzola
Associates, Inc.
Photographer: Tim Street-Porter

A FRENCH RENAISSANCE HOUSE/UNDER CONSTRUCTION
Project Architect: Suzette Smith
Architecture Team: Brian Settle, Pierre
Guettier, Akira Kurihara, Ed Watkins,
Bethany Snyder
Interior Designer: Karen Yttrup
General Contractor: Peninsula Custom
Homes
Landscape Architect: Stroudwater Design Group
Watercolor Rendering: Front facade by Brendan Hart
Precedent Image Credits:
p. 118, Fig. 1. Reproduced by permission from Hemis/Alamy.
p. 118, Fig. 2. Photograph courtesy of Cesare Gerolimetto, *Ville Venete: The Villa Civilization in the Mainland Dominion* (Verona: Arsenale Editrice, 1955), 89.
p. 119, Fig. 3. Reproduced by permission from Laurent Kruszyk, *Escaliers Parisiens sous l'Ancien Regime: L'Apogee de la serrurie* (Paris: Somogy, 2011), 172–73.
p. 119, Fig. 4. Photograph courtesy of Paige Mariucci.

A COUNTRY RESIDENCE
Project Architect: Eric Haun
Architecture Team: Matthieu Rochas,
Marianne Gruber, Lisa Marie Milat, Day
Hilborn, Jim Severson, Eliot Sutro, Jeff Eade,
Pierson Jones, Viet Truong, Natasha Juliana,
Karen Siu
Interior Designer: Steven Volpe Design
General Contractor: Peninsula Custom Homes
Landscape Architect: Todd R. Cole Landscape Architect
Photographer: Matthew Millman
Watercolor Rendering: Front facade by Brendan Hart
Precedent Image Credits:
p. 124, Fig. 2. Photograph by Paul Hayes of l'Aile des Ecuries from an original publication of *Cours d'architecture ou traité de la décoration, distribution et constructions des bâtiments contenant les leçons données en 1750, et les années suivantes,* 1771 (original publication held by the San Francisco Public Library).
p. 128, Fig. 4. Reproduced by permission from Laurent Kruszyk, *Escaliers Parisiens sous l'Ancien Regime: L'Apogee de la serrurie* (Paris: Somogy, 2011), 149.

A TOWNHOUSE

Project Architects: William Wilson, Steven Sutro
Architecture Team: Akira Kurihara, Day Hilborn, Jim Severson
Interior Designer: Tucker & Marks, Inc.
General Contractor: Forde-Mazzola Associates, Inc.
Landscape Architect: Todd R. Cole Landscape Architect
Photographer: Matthew Millman

A CITY APARTMENT IN THE HAUSSMANNIAN STYLE

Project Architect: Suzette Smith
Architecture Team: Marianne Badawi, Roger Farris
Interior Designer: Tucker & Marks, Inc.
General Contractor: Ryan Associates
Photographer: Matthew Millman
Precedent Image Credits:
p. 148, Fig. 2. Used with permission from The Biltmore Company, Asheville, North Carolina.

A NORMAN CARRIAGE HOUSE

Project Architect: Akira Kurihara
Photographer: © Steven Brooke Studios
Precedent Image Credits:
p. 154, Figs. 1 and 2. Reproduced by permission from Régis Faucon, *Manor Houses in Normandy,* (Potsdam: h.f.ullmann, 2011), 220 and 259.

A PALLADIAN ESTATE/ UNDER CONSTRUCTION

Project Architect: Akira Kurihara
Architecture Team: Nicole Bernal-Cisneros, Brian Settle
Watercolor Rendering: Front facade by Nicole Bernal-Cisneros
Detailed wing facade by Lauren Hedge
Precedent Image Credits:
p. 160, Figs. 1 and 3. Reproduced by permission of Jonathan Wallen, *The Houses of McKim, Mead & White* (New York: Rizzoli, 1998), 172–73 and 192.
p. 160, Fig. 2. Reproduced by permission from Eye Ubiquitous/ Alamy.
p. 161. © CISA A. Palladio–Vicenza

GEORGIAN ARCHITECTURE

p. 164. Detail of an Ionic column at "An Anglo-Grecian Country House." Photograph by Mark Darley

A CLASSICAL REVIVAL TOWNHOUSE

Project Architect: Ed Watkins
Architecture Team: Olivier Santoni-Costantini, Gordon L'Estrange, Kathleen Bost, Bethany Snyder, Gloria Day, Benjamin McGriff, Michael Bernard
Interior Designer: Martha Angus
General Contractor: Cove Construction
Landscape Architect: The Garden Route
Photographer: Matthew Millman
Watercolor Rendering: Front facade and front door by Brendan Hart
Precedent Image Credits:
p. 168, Fig. 1 and p. 172, Figs. 5 and 6. Reproduced by permission from John M Hall Courtesy of CAHPT, *Adventures with Old Houses* (New York: Classical American Homes Preservation Trust, 2005), 60 and 146–47.
p. 168, Fig. 2. Reproduced by permission from Peter Bennett/ Ambient Images.
p. 172, Fig. 3. Reproduced by permission from Acanthus Press, *Parallel of the Classical Orders of Architecture* (New York: Acanthus Press, 1998). Plate 23.

A COLONIAL COUNTRY HOUSE

Project Architects: David Buergler, r. Mark Rushing
Architecture Team: Robert Colarusso, Michael Callison, Sarah Kaplan, Eric Haun, Karen Siu, Natasha Juliana, Heather Hart, Marianne Badawi
General Contractor: Tincher Construction
Landscape Architect: Mai Arborgast
Photographer: Mark Darley
Andrew Skurman, p. 186, Fig. 6, carriage house door detail
Watercolor Rendering: Front and rear facades by Brendan Hart
Precedent Image Credits:
p. 181, Fig. 1. Reproduced by permission from Acanthus Press, *Parallel of the Classical Orders of Architecture* (New York: Acanthus Press, 1998), plate 18.
p. 181, Fig. 2. Photograph by Paul Rocheleau. Image courtesy *The Magazine ANTIQUES* (New York: BMP Media Holdings, LLC., July 1986).
p. 181, Fig. 3. *Great Georgian Houses of America, Vol. 2* (Mineola, New York: Dover Publications, 1970), 46.

AN AMERICAN COUNTRY HOUSE
Project Architects: Jeff Eade, Natasha Juliana
Architecture Team: Robert Colarusso, Michael Callison
General Contractor: Bridger Construction
Photographer: David Duncan Livingston
Watercolor Rendering: Outdoor pavilion drafted by Lauren Hedge and painted by Brendan Hart
Precedent Image Credits:
p. 198, Fig. 5. Pavillon des fleurs, Marly. Watercolor on paper © 1997 Edward Andrew Zega and Bernd H. Dams, Architectural Watercolors, Paris, France.

A DUPLEX PENTHOUSE APARTMENT
Project Architect: William Wilson
Interior Designer: Fisher Weisman
General Contractor: Ryan Associates
Photographer: David Duncan Livingston
Precedent Image Credits:
p. 205, Fig. 2. Reproduced by permission from © Roberto Schezen/Esto, *The Splendor of France: Chateaux, Mansions, and Country Houses* (New York: Rizzoli, 2004), 280.
p. 207, Fig. 4. Reproduced by permission from Acanthus Press, *Parallel of the Classical Orders of Architecture* (New York: Acanthus Press, 1998), plate 20.
p. 207, Fig. 5. Reproduced by permission from © Country Life, *The Country Houses of Robert Adam: From the Archives of Country Life* (London: Aurum Press, 2008), 116–17.

A GEORGIAN COTTAGE
Project Architect: Kathleen Bost
Architecture Team: Michael Callison, Ed Watkins, Marianne Badawi, Benjamin McGriff, Gloria Day, Lisa Zhou, Timothy Blanchard
Interior Designer: Tucker & Marks, Inc.
General Contractor: Lencioni Construction
Landscape Architect: Thomas Klope Associates, Inc. Landscape Architecture and Planning
Photographer: Matthew Millman
Watercolor Rendering: Front facade by Lauren Hedge
Precedent Image Credits:
p. 210, Fig. 1. Reproduced by permission from Van Jones Martin, *Edward Vason Jones 1909–1980: Architect, Connoisseur, and Collector* (Savannah, GA: Golden Coast Pub Co, April 1995), 80–81.

A CITY RESIDENCE
Project Architects: Heather Hart, Eric Haun
Architecture Team: Lisa Zhou, Karen Siu, Sarah Appleman, Natasha Juliana, Benjamin McGriff, Steven Wong, Yilin Lu, Michael Bernard, Gloria Day, Kristen Sardina, Erika Perez-Rubio, Marianne Badawi
Interior Designer: Suzanne Felson collaborated with her friend and interior designer Ken Fulk in developing the interior finishes and décor
General Contractor: Lencioni Construction
Landscape Architect: Elizabeth Everdell Garden Design
Photographer: Jade Studios, San Francisco
Watercolor Rendering: Front facade by Lauren Hedge
Precedent Image Credits:
p. 218 and p. 220, Fig. 3. Photograph © Richard Cheek, *The Work of William Lawrence Bottomley in Richmond* (Charlottesville: University Press of Virginia, 1985), 42 and 40.

AN ANGLO-GRECIAN COUNTRY HOUSE
Project Architects: Ed Watkins, Roger Farris
Architecture Team: Pierre Guettier, Kathleen Bost, Eric Haun, Sarah Appleman, Kristen Sardina, Marianne Badawi, Bethany Snyder, Francisco Matos
General Contractor: Kevin Raph & Associates
Photographer: Mark Darley
Watercolor Rendering: Front facade by Lauren Hedge
Entrance hall by Brendan Hart
Precedent Image Credits:
p. 228, Fig. 1. Andrew Wyeth. *Christina's World.* 1948. Tempera on gessoed panel, 32 1/4 x 47 3/4". Purchase. The Museum of Modern Art, New York, NY, U.S.A. ©Andrew Wyeth.
Digital Image © The Museum of Modern Art/Licensed by SCALA/Art Resource, NY.
p. 228, Fig. 2. *Early Victorian House Designs* (Mineola, New York: Dover Publications, 2006), Design X, plate 31.

BACKMATTER
p. 253. "A Mediterranean Villa" by Andrew Skurman Architects. Photograph by Suzanne Tucker
p. 254. Photograph by Kit Morris.
p. 256. Acroterion at "A Greek Villa." Photograph by Mark Darley.

BIBLIOGRAPHY

Appleton, Mark. *George Washington Smith: An Architect's Scrapbook.* Los Angeles: Tailwater Press, 2001.

Architect's Emergency Committee. *Great Georgian Houses of America, Vol. 1 and 2.* Mineola, New York: Dover Publications, 1970.

Argan, Giulio Carlo, and Bruno Contardi. *Michelangelo: Architect.* London: Phaidon Press, 2004.

Bedford, Steven Mcleod. *John Russell Pope: Architect of Empire.* New York: Rizzoli, 1998.

Blanc, Olivier, and Joachim Bonnemaison. *Mansions of Paris.* Paris: Terrail, 1998.

Boucher, Bruce. *Andrea Palladio: The Architect in His Time.* New York: Abbeville Press, 2007.

Byne, Arthur, and Mildred Stapley. *Provincial Houses in Spain.* William Helburn Inc, 1925.

Carley, Rachel. *A Guide to the Biltmore Estate.* Asheville, North Carolina: The Biltmore Company, 1997.

Dams, Bernd H., and Andrew Zega. *VERSAILLES: The Château and Its Satellite.* Paris: Connaissance et Mémoires, 2007,

D'Angelis, Gaston, and Pierre Levallois. *Les Chateaux de l'Ile-de-France.* Paris: Hachette, 1963.

Faucon, Régis, and Yves Lescroart. *Manor Houses in Normandy.* Potsdam: h. f. ullmann, 2011.

Fletcher, Sir Banister. *Sir Banister Fletcher's A History of Architecture.* 20th ed. Oxford: Architectural Press, 1996.

French, Leigh. *The Smaller Houses and Gardens of Versailles from 1680 to 1815.* New Hope, PA: The Pencil Points Press, 1926.

Garrett, Wendell. *Classic America: The Federal Style & Beyond.* New York: Universe, 1996.

Gebhard, Patricia. *George Washington Smith: Architect of the Spanish-Colonial Revival.* Layton, Utah: Gibbs Smith, 2005.

Harris, Eileen. *The Country Houses of Robert Adam: From the Archives of Country Life.* London: Aurum Press, 2008.

Jenrette, Richard H. *Adventures with Old House.* New York: Classical American Homes Preservation Trust, 2005.

Johnston, Shirley, and Roberto Schezen. *Palm Beach Houses.* New York: Rizzoli, 1991.

Lambell, Ronald. *French Period Houses and their Details.* Oxford: Butterworth Architecture, 1992.

Langley, Batty. *A Pocket Edition of Treasury of Designs or the Art of Drawing and Working the Ornamental Parts of Architecture.* London: John Tiranti & Co., 1921.

Ledoux, Claude-Nicolas. *L'Architecture.* Princeton, NJ: Princeton Architectural Press, 1983.

Leiba-Dontenwill, Jean-Francois and Roselyne Bussiere. *Escaliers Parisiens sous l'Ancien Regime: L'Apogee de la serrurie.* Paris: Somogy, 2011.

Loyer, François. *Paris XIXE Siecle: l'Immeuble et la Rue.* Vanves: Hazan, 1997.

Masson, Kathryn. *Santa Barbara Style.* New York: Rizzoli, 2001.

Mitchell, William R., and Van Jones Martin. *Edward Vason Jones 1909–1980: Architect Connoisseur, and Collector.* Savannah, GA: Golden Coast Pub Co, 1995.

Monicelli, Francesco. *Ville Venete: The Villa Civilization in the Mainland Dominion.* Verona: Arsenale Editrice, 1955.

Montclos, Jean-Marie Perouse de, and Robert Polidori. *Chateaux of the Loire Valley.* Potsdam: h. f. ullman, 2008.

———. *Versailles.* New York: Abbeville Press, 1991.

O'Neal, William Bainter, and Christopher Weeks. *The Work of William Lawrence Bottomley in Richmond.* Charlottesville: University Press of Virginia, 1985.

Palladio, Andrea. *The Four Books of Architecture.* Mineola, New York: Dover Publications, 1965.

Ranlett, William H. *Early Victorian House Designs.* Mineola, New York: Dover Publications, 2006.

Rykwert, Joseph, and Roberto Schezen. *The Palladian Ideal.* New York: Rizzoli, 2000.

Saudan, Michel and Sylvia Saudan-Skira. *From Folly to Follies.* Geneva: Evergreen, 1997.

———. *Orangeries Palaces of Glass — Their History and Development.* Geneva: Evergreen, 1994.

Schezen, Roberto. *Italian Splendor Great Palaces, Castles and Villas.* New York: Rizzoli, 2004.

———. *Spanish Splendor: Great Palaces, Castles, and Country Homes.* New York: Rizzoli, 2004.

———. *The Splendor of France Chateaux, Mansions, and Country Houses.* New York: Rizzoli, 2004.

Venditti, Arnaldo. *Loggia Del Capitaniato (Corpus Palladianum, Vol.4).* University Park, PA: Pennsylvania State University Press, 1972.

Vian des Rives, Régis. *La Villa Kerylos.* Paris: Editions de l'Amateur, 1997.

Von Mauch, Johann Matthaus. *Parallel of the Classical Orders of Architecture.* New York: Acanthus Press, 1998.

Ware, William R. *The American Vignola.* Mineola, New York: Dover Publications, 1994.

White, Samuel G. and Elizabeth. *McKim, Mead & White: The Masterworks.* New York: Rizzoli, 2003.

———. *The Houses of McKim, Mead & White.* New York: Universe, 2004.

ACKNOWLEDGMENTS

One of the most thrilling aspects of architecture is that it involves the collaborative effort of many. This book wouldn't have been published without their participation.

I thank first and foremost all of my dear clients, who entrusted me to help them create the houses in which they will live and thrive.

I thank my staff, past and present, for their participation in the various projects on which they worked. Their talent and dedication are essential contributions, especially those of our studio director Akira Kurihara and the senior project architects Pierre Guettier, Suzette Smith, and Ed Watkins, without whom these projects would not have been realized.

Special thanks to Paul Hayes. He arrived at my office fresh from the University of Notre Dame. His literary gifts, organizational skills, and theoretical knowledge of architecture have been a constant contribution in the making of this book. Thanks to Nicole Bernal-Cisneros, Brendan Hart, Paul Hayes, Lauren Hedge, Akira Kurihara, and Brian Settle for their beautiful watercolor studies and drawings.

I have known Doug Turshen since we were in school together at Carnegie Mellon. He not only made this book visually beautiful, but successfully conveyed my intentions as the author through his layouts, choices, and sequencing of the images. Doug and his associate David Huang added an important layer to the making of this book. My hat goes off to them.

Thanks to my agent Jill Cohen, who not only guided me through this process but also made the connection with the publisher that I was hoping for, Princeton Architectural Press. I thank my publisher Kevin Lippert, my editors Jennifer Lippert and Dan Simon, and everyone at Princeton for believing in this book and making it such a pleasurable experience.

I thank Diane Dorrans Saeks who with her golden pen helped me with the first stages of the conception of this book.

I have been fortunate to collaborate with interior designers who have made the houses I have designed beautiful and taught me so much in the process: Suzanne Tucker and Tim Marks, who recognized my potential and with whom I did my very first residential projects when I established my own office; Naomi Ramsden, who was very kind to introduce me to them; and the many talented associates in the Tucker & Marks office with whom I have worked with closely over the years.

I have also enjoyed collaborating with Martha Angus, Rebecca Bradley, Allison Caccoma, Nina Campbell, Diane Chapman, Orlando Diaz-Azcuy, William Diamond, Douglas Durkin, Andrew Fisher and Jeffry Weisman, Pauline Feldman, Ken Fulk, Joel Hendler, Kay Lang, James Marzo, Brian Murphy, David Phoenix, Barbara Scavullo, Darrel Schmidt, David Stonesifer, Olivier Thual, Steven Volpe, Kendall Wilkinson, Bunny Williams, Paul Vincent Wiseman, and Karen Yttrup.

I thank my wife Françoise, without her support and encouragement this book wouldn't have happened. My son Luke Skurman, whose personal success in business is an inspiration to me; my step-children Emmanuel Eytan and Raphaëlle Muhlmann-Eytan, and David Muhlmann; and my daughter-in-law Natalia Skurman, who along with Luke and my parents contributes to a very happy family life.

All of the above have accompanied me on my journey.

Andrew Skurman

A Mediterranean Villa

BIOGRAPHY

ARCHITECT ANDREW SKURMAN FOUNDED his firm in San Francisco in 1992. As principal and owner of Andrew Skurman Architects, he focuses on superbly crafted custom houses that are perfectly and logically planned to the specific requirements and wishes of his clients. His expertise lies in the elegant and refined expression of classical architecture and the interpretation of French, Georgian, and Mediterranean styles.

Skurman has received the honor of being named a Chevalier of Arts & Letters by the Minister of Culture of France. He is an appointed member of the prestigious Council of Advisors of the National Institute of Classical Architecture and Classical America. He currently serves as Creative Director of the San Francisco Fall Antique Show.

Skurman is currently designing projects in Northern and Southern California, New York, Nevada, France and China. He holds architectural licenses in California and in New York, and resides in both San Francisco and Paris.

Skurman received his Bachelor of Architecture in 1976 from Cooper Union in New York City and subsequently worked at some of the most prestigious architectural firms in the world. He began his design career apprenticing with the New York firm of I. M. Pei & Partners from 1976 to 1980. He then worked in the San Francisco office of Skidmore, Owings & Merrill as a Senior Associate from 1980 to 1987 and then as a Studio Director at Gensler and Associates in both San Francisco and Los Angeles until 1992.

Homes designed by Andrew Skurman Architects have been featured in numerous publications such as *Architectural Digest*, *House & Garden*, *Southern Accents*, *Maison Française*, *The New York Times Magazine*, *Western Interiors*, *California Homes*, *California Home & Design*, *C Magazine*, *San Francisco Magazine*, *This Old House*, *The Robb Report*, *Luxe. Interiors + Design*, *House Beautiful*, *Traditional Home*, and *Gentry Design*. Work by the firm is also included in the books *Napa Valley Style* (2003) by Kathryn Masson and *San Francisco Style* (2004) by Diane Dorrans Saeks.